Praise for
The G

I was deeply moved as I read *The Grace of Rain*. Manton has a genius for combining poetry with personal reflection and spiritual challenge. A delightful resource that will quiet your busy mind, ease your frantic heart, and bless your soul. I loved it.
— Diana Pavlac Glyer, Professor of English and author of *The Company They Keep* and *Bandersnatch: C. S. Lewis, J. R. R. Tolkien, and the Creative Collaboration of the Inklings.*

In the Grace of Rain Kirk Manton has given us a treasure trove of thoughtful, playful, open poems, poems that will reward repeated reading and perhaps help us see the grace, not only of rain, but of so much else we take for granted. He has also given his readers some rich and original ways to turn poetry into prayer, this is a very helpful book.
— Malcolm Guite, English poet, Anglican priest, singer-songwriter, and academic. Bye-Fellow and Chaplin, Girton College, Cambridge and author of *Parable and Paradox* and *Mariner: A Voyage with Samuel Taylor Coleridge*

Kudos to Kirk Manton for helping to revive the devotional in all its glory. Kirk not only provides us with accessible and meaning-filled poems that cut to the heart; he shares with us the struggles and victories that led him to compose the poem and provides helpful tips for applying the poem, and relevant biblical verses, to our own spiritual growth. May the grace in these poems and stories rain down on you.
— Louis Markos, Professor in English and Scholar in Residence, Houston Baptist University; author of *Restoring Beauty: The Good, the True, and the Beautiful in the Writings of C. S. Lewis* and *On the Shoulders of Hobbits: The Road to Virtue with Tolkien and Lewis.*

Kirk Manton is a gift. He is given to us as one who shows us how to see the glory of God in His Creation. He is a man alive with the presence of God. St. Thomas Aquinas teaches us that humility opens the eyes of wonder and that wonder opens the soul to reality. Kirk Manton has the humility to see with the wonder that opens the soul. He sees because he is on his knees.
— Joseph Pearce, Director of the Center for Faith and Culture at Aquinas College; author of *Flowers of Heaven: One Thousand Years of Christian Verse* and *The Quest for Shakespeare.*

The Grace of Rain by Kirk Manton is an invitation to experience the holiness and wonder of what we so often think is simply 'ordinary' – the present moment. With the skill of a poet, the humility of a sojourner, and the compassion of a shepherd, Manton introduces us afresh to the feel and taste of grace in a way that is immediate, intimate, and enduring. To walk through this book and come out on the other side is a pilgrimage that brings us face to face with the goodness already present in our lives, and a readiness to receive what is yet to come!
— Lancia E. Smith, Host of *Cultivating the Good, the True, and the Beautiful,* Founder of The Cultivating Project

In *The Grace of Rain,* Kirk Manton has given us a powerful, accessible and artful tool for spiritual transformation in the image of Christ. His poetry slips behind our defenses and resistances to see life through a different prism – that of God's gracious transforming reign. He accomplishes this by unpacking the spiritual and emotional movements in his own life that lie behind his poems from the retrospective view of how God has healed and redeemed his own pain and ambiguity. In so doing, he invites us to experience the same. What a gift to all of us who aspire to follow Jesus and to be more like Him, but who often get stuck! Kirk is a wise guide and his book provides us a fresh map for getting unstuck.
— Paul Jensen, Founder and President of The Leadership Institute and Affiliate Professor of Leadership and Discipleship

at Fuller Theological Seminary. Author of *Subversive Spirituality*

THE GRACE OF RAIN

The Grace of Rain…

God is speaking.
Are we listening?
Poetry and more
to quiet the
noise.

by Kirk Manton

Extraordinary Life Publishing

Printed by CreateSpace

Extraordinary Life Publishing
14720 Sundown Trail
Amarillo, Texas 79118

ISBN-13: 978-1533166227
ISBN-10: 1533166226

To

my muse, my listener, my encourager—

my wife, Rachelle

THE
SHAPE OF RAIN

If your film is fast enough
To catch a raindrop in its fall
You might be surprised to find
It's not a teardrop after all

o

Contents

Foreword

In *The Grace of Rain* Kirk Manton has given us a treasure
trove of thoughtful, playful, open poems. Poems that will
reward repeated reading and perhaps help us see the grace, not
only of rain, but of so much else we take for granted.

Shakespeare tells us that in poetry,

'as imagination bodies forth
The forms of things unknown, the poet's pen
Turns them to shapes and gives to airy nothing
A local habitation and a name.'

Kirk has the knack again and again of taking something
apparently ordinary and every day; the fall of rain, a car rusting
in a field, an ageing maintenance man looking after an ice rink,
the skaters on the rink itself, and making these things the 'local
habitation' the 'name' or symbol, for our states of mind, our
devotions, our intentions. Readers of this book will not only be
able to return to these images and find a little more packed into
them each time, but also they will find that reading poetry like
this helps them to train their own vision. Seeing how Kirk has
observed the world around him and found that every image and
picture, held up to the right light, can speak of God, or of our
need for God, can help his readers to see things in a new way
themselves, help them to see everywhere in their own lives
these sudden emblems of grace.

There are short poems here that transfigure everyday objects
and there are longer poems that take us on a journey, a journey
back through our own history, back through the bible or out
into a new appreciation of the beauty and power of God's
creation. There are poems that reveal the brief grace in little

things and poems that remind us of the awesome, indeed Angelic powers behind all the appearances of nature.

Though there is much more here than just pious sentiment, Kirk doesn't duck the big issues, or the controversial ones in this poetry. There is plenty to challenge the reader who is struggling with temptation, to provoke the reader who has become blasé or over-confident, and to rouse in every reader that sense of child-like awe and wonder which we so often lose as adults but which poetry can help to restore.

Kirk has also provided his readers, in the 'Behind' and 'Between' sections that follow the poems, a helpful resource for deepening the way they read and for making the transition between poetry and prayer. I would commend this book not only for personal use but also as a resource for small church groups or circles of friends who could read, discuss, and pray through it together.

I hope you enjoy reading these poems as much as I did.

Malcolm Guite

Acknowledgements

This book was born out of my life; a life written by relationships and groups of deep friends—it is to you all I owe my thanks for *The Grace of Rain*.

Thank you to the Crystal Cathedral, Dan Webster and the Thursday Night youth ministry family, to Bud and Kathy Pearson, Gene Ehmann, and the staff and family of Orange Coast Community Church for such a good start in the faith. To my beloved OCCC youth ministry—the staff (Lauree, Meg, David and Mark), students and DPS brothers who have kept the faith and have stayed my dear friends. Thank you to Paul Jensen and Chuck Miller, my early ministry mentors and friends. To my oldest, always there, always honest, "through-it-all" friend, Ralph Linhardt, thanks.

Thank you to my co-workers in the "glamorous" freelance film business—thanks for passing on the secrets of the craft and more importantly your friendships (especially Gus, Tom and Scotty). Thank you, my adopted home town of Amarillo, Texas, the staff and crew at the Civic Center, Marriage Today, and my Trinity Fellowship Church. Y'all welcomed this California transplant with open arms and I am so grateful. Keep up the good work, my young friends at the Amarillo Filmmakers Collective—Matt and Blake, you are so inspiring. Clint, your friendship and encouragement is priceless to me.

Thank you to those many friends who are directly responsible for my writing. My deepest thanks to Wayne and Meg Brazil, you both got me started. Your impact on my whole life cannot be overstated. Years later, all my dear friends at the C.S. Lewis Foundation, especially Stan, Malcolm and Lou, you started me writing poetry again. To Melanie Stiles, my editor and coach (you are amazing), to Frank Sobey (your mentoring in the poetic set me on course), to Jean Triggastad, my proofreader, to Nan Rinella my collaborator, to my dear friends Steven and

Lancia, and to the Pencilbiters, thank you. To the Artists on Our Knees; Blake, Matt, Daniel, Clint, Gina and Ryan your encouragement kept me going. To Alicia Cartrite your flair brings beautiful thoughts to life!

And finally, thank you to my encouraging family; to my Mother for modeling a steadfast faith, to my Father for teaching me the power of a story well told, to Eric and Lisa, my siblings deepened in Jesus, to my beautiful, intelligent and inspiring daughters: Nicole, Abree and Stefanee, my amazing son, Chris, and my sweet wife, Rachelle ("Jesus wins")— Thank You.

Introduction

———— o ————

Why Devotional ?

Why Poetry ?

Why More ?

Why Devotional?

Because *God is speaking*

Why choose the devotional genre for a book of poetry? Because I believe it to be the most important activity of Man. Why? Because devotional time with God can influence everything we do, more than anything else we do. Over time as we purposely draw our attention to God to listen, to hear, to surrender and fall in love with Him, we are transformed.

All writing, all painting, all songs and, indeed, all of life is, or can be, devotional. All art forms require attentiveness and curiosity to draw out all the fullness of what the artist is trying say.

A devotional approach to poetry can uniquely bring the joy of discovering unintended treasure which the author never intended, but God did. He can bring out hidden connections between the words and the life only you have lived. When those moments occur, you will not remain the same.

Experiencing those divine personal revelations through poetry and other art forms can prepare us for opportunities. If we choose to listen, they can come to us through every day scenes, sent directly from the Author of Life. Living with devotional awareness and expectation makes a difference.

My Story

Catching fire. In my mid-to-late twenties, my career was on the rise. I was a youth pastor in Southern California—destined for youth pastor stardom. I had the right skills, the right connections, the right resume and I was in the right place at the right time.

It all started back in high school. I caught the fire for youth ministry, while I was a student in one of the most exciting church youth programs on the west coast. It was based on the explosive "Son City" student program, lead by a young, up and coming minister, named Bill Hybels. The group later became the core of one of the largest and most influential churches in the United States.

Hooked. During my freshman year in high school, our modest group was taken over by a dynamic young man named, Dan Webster. He had caught the vision from Bill Hybels and within a year, every Thursday night, we were bursting the seams of our 400 seat auditorium. We split to two nights and kept growing. God was on the move, and for the next four years, I was hooked.

By my junior year I was a student leader in the program and dropped my promising high school sports career in water polo and swim team to devote more time to that exciting ministry. After graduating, I started studying at a local Christian college—with the goal of becoming a youth pastor myself. I was on my way.

Something missing. Three semesters into college, I was hired as a part-time youth pastor in a small Southern California church. The church had just a few teenagers, but that was fine. I was eager to get started and had a program ready to go. Within a year or so we were up to fifty kids. Not bad for a church of under 200 members! We were reaching out to the students in the neighborhood and many of them were finding new life in Jesus but I was about to burn out like a Roman candle.

I was trying to go to school full time, build a big youth ministry and start a family, all at the same time. Even though I was doing a good job at all three, something was missing, and the void was taking its toll.

Relief came. Into my hectic, driven, successful, and fragile world came new hope. God brought a few wise ministry veterans into my life. They introduced me to a devotional life of intimacy with a personal God who desperately loved me and wanted me to experience Him in a deeper refreshing way every day. One of those men, Chuck Miller, taught and modeled how through a devotional perspective I could be "guided by Biblical priorities rather than be driven by cultural pressure" (even the cultural pressures of the modern church). Another, Paul Jensen, showed me how to walk in the lifestyle rhythms of solitude, prayer and listening as modeled for us by Jesus. Relief had come.

One particular moment, during those restorative years, stands out in my mind most vividly. As part of a workshop, being taught by Paul, on developing personal intimacy with Jesus, we were to spend two hours alone in a park meditating on the familiar story of Mary and Martha in Luke 10:37-42

Now as they were traveling along, He entered a village; and a woman named Martha welcomed Him into her home. She had a sister called Mary, who was seated at the Lord's feet, listening to His word. But Martha was distracted with all her preparations; and she came up to Him and said, "Lord, do You not care that my sister has left me to do all the serving alone? Then tell her to help me. But the Lord answered and said to her, "Martha, Martha, you are worried and bothered about so many things; but only one thing is necessary, for Mary has chosen the good part, which shall not be taken away from her." (Luke 10:37-42 NASV)

Paul provided us with a list of prompting questions.

Unexpected moment. I was already familiar with the passage—had even taught on it myself. But during this devotional time—
this extended, quiet and alone time with God—something was different. I still remember—as clear as day—God saying to me,

"I love you more than what you can do for me."

I repeated the phrase over and over again to myself. Jesus was talking directly to me—personally. Through my tears I kept hearing Jesus say, "Kirk, I love you, more than what you can do for me".

It was in devotional times like these that God began touching, reviving, strengthening and maturing me in a whole new way.

Reaping. Through all my successes, victories and good times, as well as my many seasons of heartbreak, failure and deep pains, it has been my intimacy with Jesus forged in consistent, creative, devotional times with Him that has sustained and grown me. That, in some small way, is what I would like to pass along through this book.

Why a devotional? Because God is speaking, and we need to be listening.

Why Poetry?

Because *poetry can quiet the noise.*

Listening deeper. Poetry, by its very nature, can put us in the posture of listening for a deeper voice. I find poetry captures my attention, focuses my soul (mind, will and emotion), and quiets the noise around me. It can hold my gaze on an image, through which God often speaks. When I am attentive, poetry often brings joyful moments of discovery and emotional connection. Distractions fall away and I hear Him more clearly.

Through a poem, memories evoked by a line, or a word, can remind me of a message He conveyed to me years ago. I am often prompted by those memories to take action now—poetry is powerful that way.

Unlikely Hollywood introduction. Back in the late eighties I discovered the potential power of poetry as a devotional tool in the hands of God through, of all things, a Hollywood movie.

The Dead Poet Society is a coming of age story about a group of students whose lives are changed because they catch a passion for life from their teacher, who shared with them his love of poetry. The quote from the film that impacted me the most was from a poem by Henry David Thoreau,

"I went to the woods because I wished to live deliberately, to front only the essential facts of life, and see if I could not learn what it had to teach, and not, when I came to die, discover that I had not lived… I wanted to live deep and suck out all the marrow of life…"

That passage moved me deeply. It put into words the passion of my growing devotional life with Christ. I was pursuing intimacy with Jesus, seeking "to live deliberately," so that I could be led by Him and "not, when I came to die, discover that I had not lived." I wanted to "live deep and" draw from life all the Author of Life had for me. I took this passion to heart and made it the theme of a small group of high school student leaders in my youth ministry. We called the group DPS. Those boys were changed forever by the One we met in those devotional times.

Listening everywhere. In our weekly times together we read poetry, song lyrics and the Bible, discussing, praying and listening for what God had to say. We began looking everywhere for what the Lord might speak to us. This attitude of listening for His voice in the Word, literature, movies, song lyrics, etc., set in place, for us, the habit of seeing all of life as devotional.

Listening another way. Later, in a very dark and painful season of my life, a wise mentor suggested journaling and actually *writing* poetry, to help me make it through. That first poem begins this collection. *A Turning At Twilight* and other poems were angels (messengers) God used to bring me through to brighter days.

Then for a time, the fire for writing burned low, but embers remained.

Rekindled. I serve as a volunteer production manager for the C.S. Lewis Foundation. Its mission, to see a revival of Christian thought, imagination and creative expression in the academic world and the culture at large, has had a surprising effect on me. After listening behind the scenes to world class Christian artists and writers challenge their audiences to live out and express their faith through the gifts God has given them, I was inspired to begin writing for more than myself.

At the end of each day of our conferences, an opportunity was given for participants to share at an open mic. These gatherings are called "The Bag End Café" Bag End is the name of Bilbo Baggins' house in J.R.R. Tolkien's, *The Hobbit*). It was there, when I read one of my poems in public for the first time, that those old embers began to glow again.

Catching fire. During the next conference, I sat in on a poetry workshop hosted by the captivating English poet Malcolm Guite. In class, he challenged us to write a poem and come ready to share and discuss it the next day. I was not sure if the words would come again, but as I listened to God, they flowed. The next day, the experience of sharing that poem and testifying about God was liberating. I have been listening, writing and sharing ever since—the fire continues to burn.

Out of all of these experiences, this book was born. Why poetry? Because of the unique way that God speaks through verse, Poetry is well worth trying.

Why More?

Because *poetry needs to be more accessible.*

Does poetry frustrate you as much as it does me? Did you ever give up reading it because you could not understand what most poets were talking about?

Inaccessible. I have found that much of poetry's beauty, truth and gripping potential lays below the surface of unfamiliar words, characters and references. Only through challenging, time consuming study, and research could I discover what many poets were writing about, let alone what they were implying beneath the surface. If I did find the answers, it was often well worth it, but who has the time?

I have always wished that poets would include additional helpful material along with their poems. So, that is what I have chosen to do. In addition to a poem and short devotional, I have included something more—a section that I call *Behind*. This section gives the reader the backstory context for the piece and additional thoughts to help with things that might be unclear, unfamiliar or below the surface.

I strive to write poetry that is accessible and meaningful. I have written this book the way I wish other poets would.

Why poetry and more; why devotional? Because God is speaking! Life is too short not to learn to listen for His voice. It's what we were created to do. I pray that you will enjoy and grow as you soak in, *The Grace of Rain.*

Prepare For The Rain
How to read this book

One month. The booked is laid out in a traditional one-month devotional format. Most of the thirty-one chapters can be read in one sitting. Each chapter has three sections; the poem, *Behind* (backstory plus) and *Between* (devotional). If you prefer a more lingering approach, I suggest reading each chapter over three sittings—three waves.

The first wave is just the poem. Read the poem and soak in it for a while. Take this initial and listen for all God has for you. I encourage you to approach it like a Bible study. Being attentive to what it *says*, what it means (or *implies*) and then how God might have you *apply* it to your life. This is a simple Bible study method I use to teach my students. We called it CIA (Cez, Implies, Apply). Write it down. As an old mentor of mine use to say, "If your devotional time doesn't affect your calendar, you aren't listening."

The second wave is the *Behind* section. At a later time, read the back story section and re-read the poem with this new perspective. This time you may find a whole new meaning and sense new applications coming through the poem—something fresh from the Lord. It may even feel like a different poem all together—bonus!

The third wave is *Between* (you and God). This section encourages you to delve even deeper. It includes additional thoughts, questions and scripture intended to encourage additional personal intimacy with the Lord.

Prepare to take notes and share.
- Grab a notebook, computer, tablet or phone.
- Try using your favorite Bible study method or C.I.A. (above).
- Join the conversation at www.TheGraceofRain.com, share videos, music, Bible studies, insights, stories, opinions, testimonies, etc.

A TURNING AT TWILIGHT

Sun setting at his back,
hills leading home toward Jerusalem.
Rolling wave by wave before his gaze
the battle weary King
leans upon his shepherd's staff.

Oh home, oh Jerusalem,
Oh Lord God Almighty!
I long to rest in
Your arms, Your power, Your peace, Your presence.

But, out there on bloodied field and rocky hill,
where fatigue slows his sword
and terror grips him from behind,
he's not so sure.

What will tomorrow bring?
Will those on distant hill
move on us with new found strength
or falter as we charge?

Shall I sleep the victor King
in his tent tomorrow night
or cower the beaten dog,
collared to its pole?

Oh, to be home—
even as a servant,
and leave this kingly task
to younger men hungry for Your power.

I would sit at Your altar and long for You.
But You are sun and shade,
sword and shield, toil and rest.

I shall serve you here.
Long for home.
And trust You in it all.

He breathes, lingers and waits.

Cool breeze welcoming in the night,
new moon reshaping the shadows.
Behind him, one by one, the fires are lit.

Smiling, he straightens and turns,
shouldering the blade.
Back to his men he strides.

Behind

A Turning at Twilight was the first poem I ever wrote. Its original title was *A Companion to Psalm 84.* The exact dating of this poem has been, to quote one of my favorite films, *Blade Runner*, "...lost in time like tears in rain". The poem represents two very important beginnings. My first attempt at poetry and years later, the first poem I ever read aloud in public.

Late one night at a gathering of retreat attendees, staff and faculty—all on equal terms—awaited their turn at the open mic. Songs were sung, instruments played (sometimes well), mime performed and yes, poetry was read. After breathing in the steady flow of support and encouragement in the air, I gathered my courage and found this piece deep in my hard drive. I stood up to read. The experience marked for me the beginning of my real passion for writing, and reading poetry. I was hooked, undone, all in!

The original motivation behind this poem was the passion I found in Psalm 84, especially verse 10 - "I would rather be a doorkeeper in the house of my God than dwell in the tents of wickedness." The verse drew me in. I could envision David expressing passion and longing for in the presence of God—even as a servant.

Allow me to interject an additional thought about "home" from verse 10. Have you a friend, or a friend's family with whom you've felt so comfortable and safe even the mere thought of their home fills you with a sense of peace? It is a gift from God, a sign of what He wants for us in His presence.

In my Father's house are many mansions: if it were not so, I would have told you. I go to prepare a place for you. And if I go and prepare a place for you, I will come again, and receive you unto myself; that where I am, there ye may be also. (John 14:2-3 KJV)

As we understand this and grow to believe it, we will come to long for it and long for Him as David did.

On a personal note, I wrote this poem at the prompting of a good friend, who was helping me walk through one of the most difficult times of my life. I was going through a divorce and longed for home. Weariness, mistrust and lack of security weighed heavily on my heart. As I meditated on David's journey in Psalm 84, God met me in the midst of my weariness and pain and gave me the assurance that I could trust Him in it all.

———————————————— ○ ○ ————————————————

Between

For a day in your courts is better than a thousand elsewhere. I would rather be a doorkeeper in the house of my God than dwell in the tents of wickedness. (Psalm 84:10 ESV)

As the poem was birthed out of Psalm 84, I invite you to read the two pieces side by side. Listen for any parallels between the poem, the Psalm and your life. If you're going to use my CIA study template (page 25) enjoy working with any specific section of the poem God draws to your attention; listen for what it C-ez, what that I-mplies and how God is calling you to A-pply those implications to your life. Write down how God speaks to you and then, as He leads, share it with *US;* a friend, family member, or with all of *US* at TheGraceofRain.com.

———————————————— ○ ○ ○ ————————————————

THE GRACE OF RAIN

At night, when the first drops fall
on the roof and down the hall,
I hold my breath, as if to say,
Is this for real and will it stay?

The more and more the sound expands,
from me melts the worlds demands.
On any other clear, bright day
I'd strive so hard to keep my wolves at bay.

If I forget and arrive too late,
miss the mark for heaven's sake,
the stress, I might not measure up,
robs my rest with a bitter cup.

But not tonight, not the strain,
grace has come, comes with the rain.

Behind

The Grace of Rain, unlike many of my other poems, is not anchored in a specific event or geographic location. It sprang from the recurring feeling I experience when I hear first rain drops fall. It often happens when I am at home in the evening. No matter my stress about the day, when I hear those soft drops fall on the roof or against a window pane, a sensation of peace comes over me. If the sound remains and increases, my muscles relax, my concerns slowly drain away. Unconsciously, I take a deep breath, let it out and smile.

On one such evening, I began to wonder about the origin of this experience. Could I understand its root and give it a name? I came to realize that the best word to describe the feeling was grace - an undeserved, unearned favor; the sense that a reprieve has been granted.

Have you ever noticed how (for no apparent reason) people on a rainy day seem to extend more grace to each other—more patience than normal? And when there's a storm outside, have you observed even awkward social situations seem to be a little more forgiving? Even introverts have something to talk about, "Wow, how about that rain? Yeah, it's really coming down . . ." and a meaningful conversation has a chance to start.

When dark clouds are overhead and the rain's coming down in buckets, the world just seems to have more Grace. We are more forgiving and the pressure to perform seems to lessen. I like that. It reminds me of when I am worshipping and soaking in the awareness of God's love for me. God knows our weaknesses and loves us all the same. Perhaps people give each other slack during the rain because we all know we are helpless to stop the rain and the challenges it brings. Perhaps, in the rain we care for each other a little more.

Similarly, God knew there was nothing we could do about the consequences of our sin. The debt we would have to pay would be way too high. Death was the balance due. Yet His love for us compelled Him to an alternative. His painful decision on our behalf, meant the death of His Son—the only remedy for both His justice and His love. He sent His Son, Who went to the cross for us, and His grace has been raining down on us since. When it rains, our awareness of that pardoned feeling can be a reminder if we will only choose to listen.

——————————————————— o o ———————————————————

Between

The rain is a refreshing reminder of God's loving grace towards us, listen for His plea for you to extend grace toward others. Meditate on Ephesians 4:32 and *The Grace of Rain* again. Perhaps the Lord will bring to your mind someone who needs your grace, forgiveness or kindness. It may be someone who is hard to love, but needs patience, as you have needed it and received it from the Lord. Write down how the Lord would have you apply the poem and this scripture today. Then, if He calls you to, share with us at www.TheGraceofRain.com.

Be kind to one another, tender-hearted, forgiving each other, just as God in Christ also has forgiven you.
(Ephesians 4:32 NASB)

——————————————————— o o o ———————————————————

WALK IN THE REIGN

Tenderly, now take my hand.
We'll walk to where the swells meet sand.
Breath in the stars, and talk of how,
life's not as planned.

Wave by wave the memories
blow through the trees of suffering.
Recalling how the years we lost,
have been redeemed.

His presence now in every choice.
Ascribing how—a different voice.
Coming storm, or pain can't hide,
His spirit lifting deep inside.

New source is changing everything.
We're walking back, so sure of spring.
Shoes and sandals in our hands.
We've left behind the worlds demands.

When clouds now gather,
we let go of the strain,
put down our umbrella
and walk in His reign.

Behind

Walk in the Reign is the second of four poems that flowed out of my musings about rain. The other three poems are: *The Grace of Rain, Choosing Reins* and *Living Sky. Walk in the Reign* is what you might call a tasty leftover after the main course.

The simple circumstance that inspired the writing of this poem was a thought that remained after finishing *The Grace of Rain.* Often, while working on a poem, a thought or question will come to me that relates to the poem but does not quite fit within the scope of the piece. At that point, I jot a note off to the side and get back to finishing the poem at hand. When the first poem is done, I review those "left overs" and often discover that another related poem has begun.

As I enjoyed the sense of peace from *The Grace of Rain,* I found myself think of how, for my wife and I, peace has come over the years of God steadily work in us, redeeming past years of suffering and pain. Slowly as we have understood and accepted His love, His presence and His leading our trust and peace has grown.

Walking in the Reign is an exploring of the connection between the peaceful moments of *rain* and the everyday peace that grows as you let Him *reign* in every circumstance of life.

———————————————— o o ————————————————

Between

I invite you to enjoy slowly reading, line by line through the poem and the following related scriptures. Take the time to listen for what God would say to you, personally, about walking in His reign. As He leads, write down your thoughts, and then, in gratitude, record thank you notes to Him.

But if any of you lacks wisdom, let him ask of God, who gives to all generously and without reproach, and it will be given to him. But he must ask in faith without any doubting, for the one who doubts is like the surf of the sea, driven and tossed by the wind. (James 1:5-6 NASB)

Trust in the LORD with all your heart
And do not lean on your own understanding.
In all your ways acknowledge Him,
And He will make your paths straight. (Proverbs 3:5-6 NASB)

And we know that God causes all things to work together for good to those who love God, to those who are called according to His purpose. (Romans 8:28 NASB)

--- ○ ○ ○ ---

CHOOSING REINS

I

An old man helps
a little boy up
on the bench
and sits down beside him.

On his left
he stows
the bag
of borrowed books.

On his right
the little boy
wiggles in close,
opens a book
and begins to read.

Commuters gather.
They take no notice
of the two.

Why should they?
They've got
places to go.

He sees and recognizes
each one's mood—
his flesh on every face.

Why shouldn't he?
He's been
where they're bound.

Restless and cold,
the standing ones
stomp their feet,

sip their lattes,
check their watches,
and look to their left—
waiting for the 5:15.

He puts his arm
around the boy,
ponders the scene
and remembers the pain.

II

Soulish Man, he thinks he's free.
In my younger days, that was me.
"They'll never put no chains on me.
No one will tell me who to be."

Well, like the kite that cuts its string,
the ship that drops that rudder thing,
the bus empty behind the wheel,
are men that do whatever they feel.

That freedom comes at a terrible price.
It's an illusion, they never think twice.
All appetites of Man consume,
unchecked will leave them dry as a tomb.

III

Back in Eden, Man drew life from The Source.
Spirit through spirit, soul, body; the course.
Simply knowing God, not good and evil;
Man's life; God's will, a beauty primeval.

God, being Spirit, through Man's spirit could drive.
Filled all that Man was - infused, and alive;
Spirit to spirit unhindered the flow;
through wisdom, and knowledge, God guiding the grow.

Man's spirit alive, his soul found its place;
mind, will and emotions developed in pace.
Led by his spirit that draws all from God,
through soul then body to the earth that he trod.

Body, the go-between spirit/soul and the world;
taking in all the beauty God's love had unfurled.
Oh! What marvelous fusion. How wondrous to know!
Father, Son, Spirit to spirit, soul, body was so.

Remarkable trinities, what life they can know?
To creature from Creator of course would be so.
Body takes in images, sensations and sounds.
Then soul thinks, feels, chooses—astounds.

IV

Captured the attention of cherubs with awe.
All but the one, pridefully searching for flaw.
I see nothing in Man yet, for me to accuse.
But He loves the sick creatures; He'll allow them to choose.

If they choose life; stay connected with Him,
be no getting rid of them, my prospects quite grim.
But convince them, 'don't need Him', 'be like Him' instead,
with their own knowledge of good and evil—unwed.

Unwed them from Him and my ascension is sure.
His love is the virus, their rebellion the cure.
Their dependence on Him is their freedom to fly—
independence, so tempting, 'Pick freedom and die.'

Not, 'from Him', be 'like Him', kindle their pride.
Take that one, choose knowledge, lose Him and die.
There you go girl, take a bite and you'll see,
He didn't mean what He said, you'll simply be free.

Yes, now share it with him. Hey wait, what gives?
They ate the fruit, but their bodies still live.
'You said if they ate it, that day, they would die.'
Must be more to His plan, unless it's a lie.

Bodies still alive and souls still intact.
Thinking, feeling and choosing to act.
But wait, deep inside I see what He meant.
Their spirit is dead; from His it's been rent.

Well, now if they eat of the fruit of life,
they will stay like this, and end my strife.
If I can get them to taste from that fated tree,
they'll be living dead forever, no threat to me.

Now what's this I see here? I tell you He is mean.
He's putting them out. There's some kind of scheme.
Banned from the garden, got something else planned.
Protecting them still unfair in the grand.

That's ok.

Now severed from Him, they've not got a chance;
born spiritually dead, that limits their dance.
Led by their souls, they can grow, become wise.
Without His Spirit, wise in their own eyes.

With my kind of freedom, freedom from Him,
when bodies wear out, their destiny's grim.
Let the walking dead breed, fill up the earth.
My legions will see His love dead from its birth."

V

He didn't see in the garden that day,
the debt we owed, someone else would pay.
The life we lost could be born again,
no clue, the lengths grace would go to mend.

We chose our "freedom" from Him, truth, and love.
But the way was made back; cross and the Dove.
The cross paid the debt and healed the rift,
Dove brought us life, who could merit this gift?

Now Justice was served, our charge cancelled free.
No longer barred from His life giving tree.
Only two-thirds alive, with clock ticking down.
Dead spirit can live, just hand Him the crown.

Dead since the garden, crowned body and soul.
Our spirit revives as His takes its role.
His Spirit and ours united as one,
access forever, through Spirit and Son.

VI

Now who I am is more deep and secure,
deeper than body or soul, that's for sure.
Deeper than thoughts, choices or heart,
Our bodies and souls were too weak from the start.

They were created as vessels to hold
a treasure inside, more precious than gold.
God being Spirit gave spirits to man,
the means of communion, that was His plan.

Body and soul to feel, think and express
the glories of God, creation to bless.
Those parts of man would develop while led
by God, through His Spirit and our spirit wed.

What amazing grace. How sweet the Dove—
died for the ones who rejected such love.
So full is the grace that now lives inside—
patiently loving each believer to guide.

Once was 'I', now permanently 'we',
even while He's waiting for us to walk free.
Patiently waiting, if we refit old yoke—
re-heeding old lines our flesh always spoke.

Then, reminded by the Word, our pain and His voice,
"No more slave to your flesh; you have a choice."
Awakened again, we walk out with new gains.
Refreshed with true freedom—He has the reins.

VII

The bus pulls away.
He gathers the books,
helps the boy down,
takes his hand and looks

into his eyes
and answers his query.
"What? No, it's ok.
We're in no hurry.

I think we'll walk back,
perhaps through the park?
Oh, you want a story?
Plenty of time before dark.

Here's a tail worth telling,
an adventure to believe.
It starts with a couple
named Adam and Eve."

Behind

The credit for this poem goes to a good friend, Dr. Mary Pomroy Key. We were both on staff with the C. S. Lewis Foundation, working together producing conferences, special events and fundraising to found the C. S. Lewis College. During our correspondence, I sent her some early drafts of my poems. After reading *The Grace of Rain* and *Walk in the Reign,* she responded with this challenge, "Now you must write a poem about the grace of reins." The gauntlet had been thrown down and it was up to me to take up the cause.

This was a new experience for me, almost like writing a poem backwards. Usually, I start with the main idea or a scene, then the words, and then the title. This time I had the title, a key word, and perhaps a slice of an idea, but that was all. I had to listen to the Lord as to how, "reins," relates to Grace.

Writing a poem, with so little to begin, actually resulted in the longest poem I've ever written. The experience was exhilarating. The Lord led me to express, what is for me, the very heart of the gospel that changed my life.

This poem gave me the chance to wrestle with the very nature of Man, what's gone wrong with the human race and how we can get back to the true freedom, joy and meaning we were designed and created to experience from the beginning. All those many words and lines flowed from a simple, single word and a challenge from a friend. God can call such significant things out of small beginnings.

Between

His Plan – our debit cancelled and order restored.

...having canceled out the certificate of debt consisting of decrees against us, which was hostile to us; and He has taken it out of the way, having nailed it to the cross.
(Colossians 2:14 NASB)

Would you now take a moment and write down your own "certificate of debt?" Describe the choices you've made that have added to your separation from God. When you are done, lay it down before Him Visualize Him taking it away and nailing it to the cross above Jesus—"it is finished."

––––––––––––––––––––––––––– o o o –––––––––––––––––––––––––––

THE SETTING OF AN ORANGE MOON

Why did the setting of an orange moon,
so fitting for a late October sky,
surprise him so?

He did not think of settings
at that time of day.

How the world seemed upside down;
something was setting to the west of town,
while stars filled up his morning drive.

He had never thought of settings as beginnings,
perhaps that's why he feared death so.

Comforted since,
by the thought,
Perhaps THAT'S upside down, you know.

Behind

Late October 2013, I was driving to work each day very early in the morning. It was dark and the stars filled the sky - except on my left. Just above the horizon, there was the glow of a huge orange ball. Though this majestic scene surrounded me, I was not taking in the details.

My mind drifted among many other things. I watched the long straight, familiar Texas Panhandle road ahead, scanning dark parcels of land, dotted with the lights of, mostly old, mobile homes. The land to the west gently sloped downward, then gradually up again toward the horizon. On my right were houses, close up against the road. In between, a number of home businesses offered interesting services to locals.

My mind slowed down a bit as, on my left, beneath the orange glow, the scattered doublewide estates gave way to dormant, fall corn fields. They were flat and empty, save for the silent pivots waiting for spring.
At the end of Western Street, I was about to reach the only traffic light on my daily commute. With half a block to go, my gaze was drawn to the left again. Just in time, I saw the final seconds of that bright orange sphere going down behind the edge of the world. It left behind a startling glow across the bottom rim of the dark sky. A shiver passed through me as I heard myself say, "That was the moon going down, not the sun coming up."

It had not fully registered during my drive, but now that it was gone, it held my full attention. I started a mental playback through what I had just missed. A giant orange moon, so beautiful, so full and bright and so slowly going down - at the start of my day. I was startled by the sudden revelation that I had been so distracted and running on an unconscious assumption. I had missed the beauty of that ending, as a beginning.

I wondered about how many, in our world, were doing the same thing, going about their business, distracted and running on unconscious assumptions, "Days begin with risings", "Death is the end" . . . I had been startled by the moon, because I was expecting the sun, surprised that an ending was starting my day. I was moved to praise, "Thank you Jesus. You have turned death into a beginning". My next thought was, "I have to write a poem."

———————————— o o ————————————

Between

On my drive that morning I was much like the two men on the road to Emmaus, who walked with the risen Jesus without even recognizing that it was him (Luke 24:13 – 32). Oh, what a wonderful thing it is, when our eyes are finally open to see what God has for us.

They said to one another, "Were not our hearts burning within us while He was speaking to us on the road, while He was explaining the Scriptures to us?" (Luke 24:32 NASB)

Spend time exploring moments in your life when God surprised you by revealing something new and significant. Perhaps they were moments of reversals of assumptions. These could be instances when you realized, like the character in the poem, that thankfully something you believed was not true, and you were relieved it was not. May we pray for such revelation and the humility to receive it.

———————————— o o o ————————————

THE SHOW

for Patty Manton

Why are some clouds so white?
'Cause God don't paint on blue.
And on some special mornings
He's got a show for you.

Did you ever ask yourself,
in the morning light,
why the sky is blue
and clouds are white?

Well, on those "random" mornings
when all things are just right,
there are still clouds overhead
like canvas stretched last night.

And when there is a gap
over to the east,
if you take the time to wait,
get ready for a feast.

He's thrown out a soft surface,
now lays down on His back,
and if you lay down beside Him,
you'll forget about your lack.

Resist the urge to go now.
Just keep your gaze up under.
He'll slowly paint your world
and fill your heart with wonder.

Don't look away for a moment.
For if you do, it's past.

It's only for these moments
and for memories that last.

He'll fill the sky with color,
bright changing hues and darks.
God paints the underside of heaven
and fills your heart with sparks.

Why are some clouds so white?
'Cause only white can hold
colors like that crimson
and throw them back so bold.

That is why He died
and shed His blood for you.
So you'd become as white
and reflect His glory too.

Behind

It was early Sunday morning on September 15, 2013. I was leaving for work, trying to navigate between front door and screen door. Like the pages in a book, I opened the screen door with my left hand, while trailing the front door behind with my right, hoping to close it without dropping my backpack. Halfway through this comical maneuver, I stopped in my tracks. Across the porch toward the eastern horizon, I saw the beauty of the sun's rays painting the underside of the clouds. I called to my wife, "Rachelle, come and see." We stood there for a moment, silent, taking in the scene. A breath of cool morning air, a kiss and I was off to work.

As my little Honda CRX hummed along, my eyes were drawn again and again to the powerful, scene. There were clouds and colors filling the sky.

For the remainder of my five mile drive, I wrote and re-wrote, over and over in my mind, the first lines, *"Why Are Some Clouds So White?"* Once I arrived at church, I practically ran to my desk. I booted up my computer and frantically began typing. Twenty or thirty minutes later, the first draft was done.

Most of this poem is simply about basking in the joy of the gift of creation.

The poem was originally called, *"Why Are Clouds So White?"* I was moved to change the title to, *The Show*, as a tribute to my late sister-in-law, Patty Manton. Patty was diagnosed in 2009 with stage four ovarian cancer and given four months to live. God had different plans. For the next four years Patty fought, and loved and encouraged everyone around her to fall in love with Jesus and His Presence. She touched so many lives.

I had the privilege of spending some extended time with her at a family reunion on Lake Erie in Ohio, the summer before she died. Every evening she invited all of us to join her down at the shoreline to see what she called "The Show." As the sun set across the lake, God painted the sky and we would sit in silence or quiet conversation, not knowing how much longer we would be able to share together. We enjoyed The Show. It is because of and for Patty I changed the title and dedicated this poem to her.

---- o o ----

Between

Have you ever sat before some beautiful scene of nature and ask yourself the "why" and the "what" questions? "Why is that stream so happy? Why does that mountain seem so lonely? Why is this desert vista so inviting in the morning?

Or do you, perhaps, ever ask, "God, what are you trying to tell me through this thundering waterfall?" Do you even take the time to pause, look, feel, listen and ask questions at all? Look for those opportunities to pause and ask today.

For since the creation of the world His invisible attributes, His eternal power and divine nature, have been clearly seen, being understood through what has been made, so that they are without excuse. (Romans 1:20 NASB)

---- o o o ----

LIVING SKY

Rain brings heaven to us nigh.
It wakes us to the living sky.

When only still clouds mark the day,
distant stars overnight are lay.
They're frozen scenes on our earth's dome,
old snapshots of an empty home.

Distant and small, separate we feel,
left here alone, judged, no appeal.
Changes slowly, gives us no heed.
Beautiful, yes, cares not for our need.

But then comes the rain.
It welcomes me home.
The sky is alive,
and I'm not alone.

Behind

The Living Sky followed soon after *The Grace of Rain,* or to be more accurate, they overlapped each other. God reminds me of His closeness when I look up into falling rain. Somehow His presence doesn't quite feel as personal to me when I look up into a sky filled with still clouds or stars. The cool, wet touch of the rain on my face can break the spell that He is distant. If I am feeling guilty or alone, He'll sometimes use a good downpour to remind me that He has washed me clean forever - and He is always there to welcome me home.

───────────────── o o ─────────────────

Between

Can you remember a time in your life when you believed there was no God?

...remember that you were at that time separate from Christ, excluded from the commonwealth of Israel, and strangers to the covenants of promise, having no hope and without God in the world. (Ephesians 2:12)

Can you relate specifically to any of the thoughts and feelings expressed in the poem or the scripture above? Describe the feeling(s), the circumstances and what God used to bring you through that season to the place of believing and experiencing His presence. Like the rain in the poem, what does God now use in your life to remind you that He is always there, even in times when you're feeling lonely, or perhaps experiencing times of lingering doubt?

───────────────── o o o ─────────────────

SIGNS MISSED

When angels become gods, they become demons.
C.S. Lewis (paraphrase)

Her doctor says it's leg or life.
His ultimatum—porn or wife.
The cyclist chooses dope to win.
What lifted up now, rots within.

While growing up, her warmest times,
family gathered round the table.
Comfortably sitting next to Dad,
catching smiles across from Mom,
listening to the boys tell their tales,
passing stories, mashed potatoes.

During celebrations, they'd set the mood
by toasting with sweet savory food.
And in-between when Mom would say,
"Such a good girl, love you this way",
they would sneak off together
for a tasty treat.

Full of promise, coming of age,
he grew up strong, handsome and kind.
On dreams of a future wife he'd thrive,
quickening his pulse, drifting his mind.

Hanging out with the guys,
he was daring and bold.
But nervous with the girls,
if truth be told.

Still, he'd fall in love,
class after class;
crushes on teachers,
Pam as she passed,

Then cheerleaders
and shy pretty things.
They'd catch his fancy
and his heart would sing.

Winning came early,
first at thirteen.
Three years later gone pro.
What a rush of esteem.

By nineteen,
two-time national champ.
Victories and sponsors,
kept raking them in.

But at twenty-five, cancer overtook.
In front of the world, defeated that foe
Came back and beat the tour
seven times in a row.

As she grew older
and her family apart,
she coped with the pains

of an empty heart.

Turning and returning
to the comfort she knew,
that led to pricking her finger
three times a day.
Choosing the right dose,
so alive she'd stay.

But now, that's not enough,
an amputation is due.

Before he grew out
of crushes and "scary."
Before the courage
to date and to marry,

he found heart pounding pictures
beyond dreams he knew,
and bought the world's lie--
"No harm in preview."

"I'll stop after the wedding", he told himself.
But habits are hard to put on the shelf.
Wagon cuts become ruts, year upon year.
Even with the vow, they don't disappear.

Marriage was rougher than a young man thought.
Back into comfort from fantasy bought.
Then she found his stash, felt crushed and betrayed.
Alone now, price of the lie to be paid

Once at the top, to what lengths would he go?
To stay the world's best, he'd risk the whole show.
Race after meaning, through glory and fame,
cheat to compete and he peddled to shame.

Every sin, man's pure desire bent.
Every wound, provision falsely spent.
Every idol, pleasures purpose missed.
Every demon, angel once, now upraised fist.

When signs are taken for destinations,
No traveler makes it home.

Behind

Signs Missed actually started out as a very short poem. It was to be the first poem in a series of three inspired by the theme and messages of a C.S. Lewis Foundation retreat I attended during the fall of 2010. The three poems are included in this book under the titles, *Signs Missed, The Cause* and *Back to Joy*. The theme of the retreat was Heaven.

At this point, you might be saying to yourself, "Hey wait a minute, none of those three poems talk about heaven. How could that theme have been their inspiration?" The four lectures that influenced me the most related how God reveals His nature. There are "signs" of heaven everywhere. The lectures lead me to consider what happens when those signs are missed.

Signs Missed originally was composed in its entirety from these six lines,

Every sin, man's pure desire bent
Every wound, provision falsely spent
Every idol, pleasure's purpose missed
Every demon, angel once, now upraised fist

When signs are taken for destinations,
No traveler makes it home.

I still enjoy this short version, but in order to help the poem stand on its own, and to better communicate the depth of the message, I expanded the poem to include examples—three painful stories.

May we all learn to see the signs pointing to Him; then listen, trust and follow.

—————————————— o o ——————————————

Between

As you begin your devotional time with, *Signs Missed*, why not linger on the epigraph (the line before the poem begins) and its familiar characters: angels, gods and demons.

Angel – the word in Hebrew (mal'ak) means: one sent, messenger or representative. In Greek, the word sounds more familiar, it is "aggelos" and means a messenger, envoy; one who is sent.

Demons - fallen angels, those angels who rebelled against God and are in league with Satan. Metaphorically, anything we allow to hinder our life spiritually, physically, emotional, or mentally; that which works to devour us.

How many people and circumstances in our lives are angels, sent to convey something from God? As representatives or envoys, they are here on behalf of someone else, not for themselves. In the Bible the real (non-metaphorical) angels were about God's business, delivering His messages and not their own. They were never willing to be worshipped—to be seen as The Source—but, always pointed to God.

Jesus showed us how even the simplest things on earth could be seen as angels (signs) sent to teach.

But he answered, "It is written, "'Man shall not live by bread alone, but by every word that comes from the mouth of God.'" (Matthew 4:4 ESV)

Bread is like the Word of God, in that it feeds us. Food gives us what our body needs when we are hungry but cannot fulfill all of our needs. If used to sooth a hurting heart, it can mask or distract us from what we truly need. It is no substitute for deeper healing that only God can bring.

As you read, pray and listen, be attentive to what God might want to reveal to you about the "angels" in your life. What do they communicate to you about God and His relationship with you?

——————————————— o o o ———————————————

SKĪĪSLANDER

Who runs the islands' eastern shores above?
Who lights the fires that wake the morning doves?
To bid and guide the stubborn sun once more,
he brings the coast to blaze as if to war.

Then douses them again with cooling white;
buckets full of the sweet, sweet morning light.
As we all below, in the amber glow,
turn our backs on the night to face the show.

From top the darkest island's mountain chain,
he'll ride to earth the grey thin streaks of rain.
He feeds the forest veins and cracks the rocks,
wets dusty planes, and quenches thirsty flocks.

In green or white or blue or flowing brown,
he covers all when true his charge comes down,
and yes, was gentle with the flowing brook,
but fierce when towers in the tempest shook.

And how! the watcher of the firmament,
the keeper for the Crown, he is content,
sustaining the Redeemer's treasured world
since Noah's drowned and slowly His unfurled.

He quietly comes down in rain or mist,
then does return at will when warm sun's kissed
the cool clear water from which vapors rise
the steward to his islands in the sky.

As islands drift apart and waves of light
rush in so bold, their piercing streams so white,

he firmly tames the beams and rips the seams
through droplets are the hidden colors seen.

Then bends them to His will, into a bow,
the Father's pledge from ancient days to show;
the promise rain won't stop another day
from rising bright upon his eastern bay.

When day is spent and orange sun is bent
on leaving tired earth to sleep content,
the Skīīslander, he sits on western shores,
and reaches down to show us all one more.

The changing light that trails the sun to bed
he splits and paints the waiting sky with red
and amber tails that glow so fiery bright,
a warning that will usher in the night.

And so the silent seraph does the tell,
so as to draw to love and keep from hell.
God cleanses the earth when our evil is dire—
the first time water, but the next time fire.

Until that day when all is made anew,
he boldly reigns the skies for me and you.
His message; man can trust the One he serves.
Heed what He said, He always keeps His words.

Behind

The journey of writing *Skūslander* started at sunrise on my front porch swing. From there I traveled through the changing colors of the sky-island clouds over head. These bold scenes led me to thinking of a burly Norse god character that might be behind them all. As the morning progressed, and the stanzas came, the "Thor" became a "Gabriel," and I imagined the extraordinary life of an angel who, tasked by His creator, stewards the heavens and the bounty they contain.

Reflecting on this mighty seraphim's charge and temperament, I found myself hearing, anew, those ancient messages etched in the Word. Those warnings and promises that are borne in the elements of water and fire:

The Rainbow Promise

I set My bow in the cloud, and it shall be for a sign of a covenant between Me and the earth. "It shall come about, when I bring a cloud over the earth, that the bow will be seen in the cloud, and I will remember My covenant, which is between Me and you and every living creature of all flesh; and never again shall the water become a flood to destroy all flesh.
(Genesis 9:13-15 NASB)

The Warning of Fire

But by His word the present heavens and earth are being reserved for fire, kept for the day of judgment and destruction of ungodly men. ... But the day of the Lord will come like a thief, in which the heavens will pass away with a roar and the elements will be destroyed with intense heat, and the earth and its works will be burned up.
(2 Peter 3:7, 10 NASB)

All Will Be Made New

And I saw a new heaven and a new earth: for the first heaven
and the first earth were passed away . . .
(Revelation 21:1 KJV)

I am watchful now, for we can daily see this Skiislander's
hidden hand; protecting, providing and prophesying that, *God
always keeps His words.*

---○ ○---

Between

God used the poets of the Old Testament to tell us how He is
always speaking to us through His creation.

"But now ask the beasts, and let them teach you;
And the birds of the heavens, and let them tell you.
Or speak to the earth, and let it teach you;
And let the fish of the sea declare to you.
Who among all these does not know
That the hand of the LORD has done this,"
(Job 12:7-9 NASB)

The heavens declare the glory of God,
and the sky above proclaims his handiwork.
Day to day pours out speech,
and night to night reveals knowledge.
There is no speech, nor are there words,
whose voice is not heard.
Their voice goes out through all the earth,
and their words to the end of the world.
(Psalm 19:1-4 ESV)

God has promised that the Holy Spirit, who in us, will help
reveal to us what He is saying.

"But when He, the Spirit of truth, comes, **He will guide you into all the truth**; for He will not speak on His own initiative, but whatever He hears, He will speak; and He will disclose to you what is to come.
(John 16:13 NASB)

As you go about your day, today, as you are outside in God's nature, under God's firmament, be attentive and ask the Holy Spirit to reveal to you what God is personally saying to you through what you see. Take notes as if all of today is one continuous devotional time with the Lord, for that is truly what it is.

—————————————————— o o o ——————————————————

BACK TO JOY

Down the stairs
my nephew flies.

The day is here,
it's finally arrived.
He knew it would, he had no doubt.
He knows what Christmas is all about.

He weaves his way through hips and thighs,
lifted elbows and judging eyes.

For him, all other celebrations,
they're practices
and preparations,
little Christmas imitations.

Knees hit the carpet before the tree,
small eyes and fingers darting free.

At times it must have seemed far off,
this little guy, he never scoffed.
Distracted perhaps by summer and school,
then pumpkins, turkey and the weather got cool.

Colors flashing as tags are read,
sifted, sorted and stacked instead.

Then browns and golds turned reds and greens—
colors, smells, sounds and scenes.
Christmas had come, the world made sense.
The rest of the year was mere pretense.

He sits back and grins-- job well done.
Then turns and strains to find his mum.

I've seen him at birthdays, at school and at play,
nothing compares to Christmas day.
But it's not just the presents, and not just the day;
the whole season affects him in such a deep way.

His smile returns as our eyes meet.
He motions for me to have a seat.

Where have I lost
that kind of joy,
and traded away
what I had as a boy?

My magic childhood Christmas dreams,
the confidence that there was more,
they grew into ambitious schemes,
that once achieved became a bore.
Each successive toy began
to gather dust and grime.
Mistaken for the source of joy,
they could not bear the weight of time.
But Christmas holds the promise still,
the reason we all yearn for more.
Gifts of this life cannot fulfill,
to point the way is what they're for.
When they no longer have to bear
the weight of all our longings,
gifts can be enjoyed and lead to where
in Christ are true belongings.

We adults,
we stand around,
while children live
where joy is found.

I gladly put my coffee down
and joined my nephew on the ground.

Behind

I must admit the opening line of this poem and the nephew character were inspired, not only by my own memories of Christmas, as a boy, but also by one of my favorite Christmas movies, *A Christmas Story*. That movie evokes deep feelings of nostalgia, memories of a pre-teen Kirk full of dreams and joy during the Christmas season. Like the lead character Ralphie, I dreamed of what Christmas day would bring, what heroic adventures I would have on a new bike, with a cool slot car track or, dare I say it, with my very own BB GUN.

Once I became a Christian, in my early teens, I began to better understand the sustaining joy that can be ours once we get to know the Christ that all the wonderful Christmas traditions point toward. I found a sustaining Christmas joy early and worked through the transition of adulthood with that joy still intact. I am so blessed, now, that it still flourishes each December, but I understand for many, like the uncle in the poem, those childhood dreams of Christmas fade with the innocence of childhood. When no adult understanding exists about what Jesus Himself brings, the holiday (and the rest of life) can become pretty joyless. Fortunately, Christmas comes every year. Every winter, all around the world, adults have the chance to remember and to delight in the children around them. It's a new opportunity to see the signs and to hear the Good News again.

Between

I invite you to unpack a child's joy of Christmas a bit. Ask the Lord to take you a little deeper into the root of joy and discover how it can apply to your life experience with Him today.

If your childhood Christmases were not the best of times and have not left you with fond memories, then ask the Lord to reveal other memories, outside of Christmas, that take you back to the kind of joy described in the poem.

When we are young, those connections between our stuff, our heroic fantasies, our joy and our identity can make strong, lasting impressions. As we grow older, pain, failures and shame cause those connections to become frayed, weak or distorted.

When we were small and our world was small, those gifts and relationship connections were enough to settle us into peace.

As adults, we need an anchor from Someone who really knows us. A relationship based on surface knowledge will not do. Christmas points to that Someone. We need love that is not frail from One who will never leave us, turn on us or let us down.

After you read the poem again, why not explore, with God, some of your specific childhood memories of joy and how they were related to significant people in your life.

1. List the experiences, the people and the feelings.
2. What did those experiences tell you about yourself?

––––––––––––––––––––––– o o o –––––––––––––––––––––––

WHAT IT IS…

Anyone with the right education
and a microscope
or a telescope
or even a knife,
can divide into parts,
the *secrets* of life.
Analyze, Scrutinize, and Categorize.

And tell you what it's made of—
but who can tell you what it is?

Anyone with the right degree
can dig up the find,
lay out the stones,
sift the earth,
and arrange the bones.

Pour in assumptions
till they fill in the gaps.
Draw in conclusions,
make up their own maps,
then publish their theories as if they are facts.

They can tell you what it's *made of*,
but who can tell you what *it is*?

But what does it matter—
Made of or *is*?

It's not a big deal.
It's not worth a fight.
If I can tell you what it's made of,

then I've got the right

Can the mother really decide?
Who gets the power to claim?
Fetus or Baby.
They are not the same.

One is a stage,
the other has a name.
Made of and *is*.
They are not the same.

"Ascribe to the Lord
the Glory due His name."

God gets the say.
It was His from the start.
HE tells us What It Is.
He makes more than parts.

Behind

Late one night, my thoughts were drawn to one of my favorite passages from *The Chronicles of Narnia.* I ruminated on the phrase "….that is not what a star is but only what it is made of." and my first new poem of a fresh writing season began.

The line stands out to me as a most significant invitation.

If all we are is parts, just another arranging of the same material as everything else, then who's to say we humans are of any special value, or have any purpose higher than any other random arrangement of the same kinds of parts?

Throughout history, mankind has been asking the question, "What am I?" And he wants an answer that constitutes more than what he is made of.

After two thousand years, the source of the answers is still obscured from most of the world. Our pride and the continued growing secularization of our culture has made it so. We live, learn and work within structures based on the presupposition that all that is real is what we can observe and measure. But when we rely on our own limited capabilities, our senses, intellect and the instruments we create as our only source of data and knowledge, though we may find out more and more about what a thing is made of, we will never truly discover what it is. Most tragically, we will never find out what or who we truly are.

The source of those answers has come. He is still active and accessible. The Creator has not left us alone, but provided a reliable source (the Bible) of knowledge about where we've came from, where we are going, who we are and what our value is. In the living Christ, He has made a way for us to have a relationship with Him and experience an ongoing, living connection and interaction through His indwelling Holy Spirit. He alone can tell us who we are.

Between

"Where were you when I laid the foundation of the earth? Tell me, if you have understanding. (Job 38:4 ESV)

I would like to start off my devotional suggestions for the poem, *What it is...*, by inviting you to take a day to reflect on portions of the first two chapters of Paul's first letter to the Corinthians. (start at verse 18 of chapter 1). Look for how this passage relates to what you found in the poem. The Holy Spirit, through Paul, is comparing two sources of knowledge; the "wisdom" of the world and the wisdom of God.

As you read with a listening attitude and ear, ask God to show you, any connections He might want you to draw between the two sources of knowledge in the poem and the two in the Bible.

What does God tell us about the value of man and of you?

God has a unique perspective on all things. Only God can look beyond the parts of a thing and tell what it is - what it is truly worth!

———————————————————— o o o ————————————————————

THE MYTH OF HEAVEN

If only I could find the door
If only I were born

> G.K. Chesterton

Heaven is, to our earth ears,
as our world to the unborn appears.
A crazy tale, a fairyland,
a dream, a myth, an outstretched hand.

If this be so, then we're no fools,
we-ones who dream outside the rules.
To many, heaven seems a wish,
a childhood dream to be dismissed.

Yet our world is real, as we all know,
making wise the unborn child who thinks it so.
And as the child who longs for birth,
We, too, are restless in our womb of earth.

We yearn for somewhere beyond and free,
we know is just outside—eternity.

Behind

Behind the poem, *The Myth of Heaven*, is one of my favorite poems, by one of my favorite writers, G.K. Chesterton.

I have come to love Chesterton for his witty humor, iron logic, and his masterful use of mind slapping paradox. He is one of the most interesting characters straddling the turn of 20th century

While reading through a book of his poetry, I stumbled upon a poem entitled, *By The Baby Unborn*. I was gripped by the way it re-humanized the emerging person in the womb, the person we all once were. The poem inspired me to write *The Myth of Heaven*. The two lines used as its epigraph are Chesterton's.

The image of the unborn dreaming of a world we know to be real, prompted me to explore the idea of heaven from the same perspective. *The Myth of Heaven* comes from the place where we are inquisitive on the inside, longing for the freedom of the outside. We sense that a world beyond nature is what we were made for. We long for that other world we have heard about from One who has been there, and now is there, and knows it to be true. The world of the One who made us and beckons us to come join Him when it is our time. And to those still saying, "If only I could find the door," He has already said, and is still saying, "I am the Door".

---- o o ----

Between

If Christianity is a myth that happens to be true and you are a Christian, then you too, are a true myth with your own magical story. For your devotional today, ask God to tell you a story— your story.

"This is the story of a boy (or girl) named (your name here) who started life as a _____ and his (or her) life was _____ but then one magical day..." (let God fill in the rest).

In writing your story, be mindful of the people in your life who seemed magical to you. Take note of those who helped you find your way to Him. Perhaps you'll recall some news (the gospel) that seemed too good to be true, but to your amazement worked a change within you that you could not resist.

For I consider that the sufferings of this present time are not worthy to be compared with the glory that is to be revealed to us. For the anxious longing of the creation waits eagerly for the revealing of the sons of God. For the creation was subjected to futility, not willingly, but because of Him who subjected it, in hope that the creation itself also will be set free from its slavery to corruption into the freedom of the glory of the children of God. For we know that the whole creation groans and suffers the pains of childbirth together until now. And not only this, but also we ourselves, having the first fruits of the Spirit, even we ourselves groan within ourselves, waiting eagerly for our adoption as sons, the redemption of our body.
(Romans 8:18-23 NASB)

Enjoy asking, listening, receiving, writing and please share your story with us at TheGraceofRain.com.

--------------------------------- o o o ---------------------------------

TIME

Time is now. And only for the choosing.
It's not how much you have, but how you're spending.
When you think you're saving up, you're losing.

Not a river dammed for later using.
She runs to waste, or brings to life, depending.
Time is now. And only for the choosing.

Not money banked, security pursuing.
The richest life is fragile — snap! It's ending.
When you think you're saving up, you're losing.

Not for neglect, too many abusing.
Yours will count for hurting or for mending.
Time is now. And only for the choosing.

Though it seems fast then slow, flying then cruising,
Time is in fact a steadiness unending.
When you think you're saving up, you're losing.

As it comes, must be spent, no reusing.
Living in the future, rules not bending!
Time is now. And only for the choosing.
When you think you're saving up, you're losing.

Behind

The poem, *Time*, came from a walk down an airport runway, a revisiting of my adolescent identity as "a car guy" and a challenge from a friend to write a villanelle.*

I love the uniqueness of where I live. Years ago, when all our children had left the nest, my wife and I decided to downsize and move a bit further out of the city. While driving the neighborhoods south of town in search of a new home, a "For Sale by Owner" sign caught my eye. The most curious thing about the sign was how the description of the property ended with the phrase "…runway and railroad access."

For the past eight years, I have often enjoyed going to sleep to the rhythmic hum of an iron horse locomotive passing by.

One of the numerous advantages of my much coveted runway and railroad access is the ability to take long, leisurely walks for thinking, musing and listening to God.

Early one evening, I headed out my back gate. A couple of properties down, along the edge of the grass runway, I found myself admiring a very large garage/hanger. A familiar thought was conjuring in my mind. *If only, I had a garage that big. Wow! What a car project I would have.* All of my old dreams of restoring a late 60's or early 70's British sports car came flooding back in a flash. I was mentally back in high school again.

---

* The pattern of a Villanelle – 19 lines, 6 stanzas (5 with 3 lines and the last with 4), Line 1 repeating as line 6, 12 & 18 and Line 3 repeating as line 9, 15 & 19, Line 2's ending must rhyme with the ending of lines 5, 8, 11 & 14, and all the remain line endings must rhyme with line 1. Quite a fun challenge from a friend. Thanks Rebekah Choat.

The next thing that caught my eye brought me back to the present and to the peace of who I truly am. There, in the next yard, was a late 70's model Camaro, sitting neglected in waist-high yellow grass. This was undoubtedly another car guy's dream project, waiting for space in a garage—the victim of adult realities, not enough money or, more likely, the illusion of not enough free TIME.

The sight of the car provoked a serious of questions I have entertained all my life. Not, *What can I do based on the space, money and time that I have?* But, *What do I choose to do with those things, especially, with my limited time?* It's less a matter of what I have, but more about what I value. Yes, I enjoy the car fantasies. When I think of being that guy, with the cool car, I feel fantastic. But what in my life, now, would I give up or trade to actually have that car? *Nothing.* The peace that comes with the awareness of what I have or do not have is my choice, is quite a gift.

God reminded me that what I value, I choose. It's who I am—who He's called me to be—and that is enough.

———————————————— o o ————————————————

Between

As you enjoy the poem, *TIME,* and the following scripture, I encourage you to think on how you choose to spend your hours.

"So do not worry about tomorrow; for tomorrow will care for itself. Each day has enough trouble of its own.
(Matthew 6:34 NASB)

…encourage one another day after day, as long as it is still called "Today," so that none of you will be hardened by the deceitfulness of sin. (Hebrews 3:13 NASB)

Come now, you who say, "Today or tomorrow we will go into such and such a town and spend a year there and trade and make a profit yet you do not know what tomorrow will bring. What is your life? For you are a mist that appears for a little time and then vanishes. Instead you ought to say, "If the Lord wills, we will live and do this or that." (James 4:13-15 ESV)

Walk in wisdom toward outsiders, making the best use of the time. (Colossians 4:5 ESV)

Therefore be careful how you walk, not as unwise men but as wise, making the most of your time, because the days are evil. (Ephesians 5:15-16 NASB)

Spend your devotional time exploring, with God, the connections between choice and time. What choices you can make so each of your "nows" are filled with wonder, purpose and meaning?

"If we live by the Spirit, let us also walk by the Spirit." (Galatians 5:25 NASB)

───────────────────── o o o ─────────────────────

HEROES STILL?

When I was young, and throughout my life
I've loved the tales of men ready for strife,
the kings and squires and the knights of old,
valiant stout men, who were fearless and bold.

Drawn by their virtues, to which I aspire,
courage, and strength and a passion like fire,
they'd protect the weak and vanquish the foe,
rescue the maidens, send evil below.

All this is thrilling, inspiring and fine.
But how does it apply to a life like mine?
Where are the dragons, the armies, the spells?
And where is the life of which legend tells?

If eyes could see, we live it every day.
Yes, a Kingdom's at stake. Make no delay.
Maidens held captive and dragons abound.
Armies of wizards, casting spells around.

Renewed incantations that God is dead.
An impersonal force, natural instead.
Something to be harnessed, feel or let flow,
only material, no one can know.

Not like old myths, foreshadowing the One;
Man's common longing fulfilled in the Son.
They may have been tales, but they did not lie—
pointed to meaning beyond live and die.

Don't get me wrong. Assume where I'm going,
Don't blame science for all this dark snowing.

Science knows that God is outside its sphere.
Can't measure, repeat, or review by a peer.

White-coated wizards have taken the leap,
willing men followed down, slippery and steep.
Can't measure Him, test Him, bind Him or prove—
conclude, "Nonexistent", "How we've improved."

New Profs were glad to void old shame and guilt,
happy to break down the walls God had built.
Walls to protect, boundaries to reveal,
then could repent, be forgiven to heal.

Walls that would stop us from having our fun.
They must see them down until there are none.
None of the walls that could protect and guide,
no truth boundaries, where innocent could hide.

So decades ago the battle was turned.
Evolution enthroned passions that burn.
Science and logic got stripped of their birth
by men glad to remove God from the earth.

The wizards removed the possible God,
teaching only proofs that work on this sod.
Purpose, meaning, lost to cause and effect,
now nothing exists that we can't detect.

Revelation removed as source from books.
Social science tells us who are the crooks.
What's healthy, what's normal, it's theirs to say.
Feels good, must be good, was born this way.

A few generations and we're set adrift.
Confusion and fear, to children our gift.
As our ladies stood up for things that were wrong,
but we left behind God, how far we have gone?

Since, so much racism, decades ago,
along with vices their virtues must go.
We'll redefine family, gender and rights,
while more fatherless children cry through the night.

So, how's it apply to a life like mine?
Still takes courage, strength and passion entwine.
The struggle still real, stakes still so high.
The battle, so different than meets the eye.

Now it's . . .

Courage to follow the One they reject.
Strength to lay down the self-life they protect.
Passion to pursue truth right to the end.
Heroes are still the ones bucking the trend.

Now we're the elders, will we make the choice?
Pursue truth with passion, heeding His voice.
Will we tell the youth of the knights of old?
And show them YOU; real, loving and bold.

Behind

I am quite the cinematic fan. Over the span of my life, I have watched a lot of movies. During one season of my life, I even worked on feature films as a lighting technician, a grip or a gaffer. I love being involved in the dramatic telling of a story, especially those with compelling characters struggling to achieve something of real value and significance. I am moved by characters who face physical, mental or relational challenges and persevere for a noble cause. I am inspired by those who sacrifice and overcome for those they love. I love a good hero.

I have come to realize that my favorite films have always been those rare movies that present a character whose Christianity is central to who they are. I find myself not only looking for those kinds of heroes in films, but also in history and real life.

Of all the heroes presented to us by the world, in the media and in school, where are the Christians characters I can really admire and look up to? Where are their stories, romances, struggles, and adventures? I want to hear about their defeats and victories.

A number of years back, I started an intentional search. And I was initially inspired by the movie *Chariots of Fire*. Amazingly enough, this film has a hero who was Christian and won the academy award for best film in 1981. The film tells the real life story of Eric Little, Olympic gold medalist runner, whose Christianity was the central force behind all he did. His story was amazing, far beyond where the film left off. I found my first hero truly worth admiring.

Later, other films introduced me to other world changing heroes, such as *Amazing Grace*, which is about William Wilberforce, a man who fought for over twenty years to end slavery in the British Empire. His life cause succeeded just three days before he died.

Heroes Still? was inspired by these kinds of heroes.

──────────────── o o ────────────────

Between

Having heroes can inspire us, motivate us and, hopefully prepare us to face challenges in our lives. Even if we are not facing the same extraordinary battles as our super heroes, their examples can help us deal with real struggles. On what type of heroes are you focusing?

Be imitators of me, just as I also am of Christ.
(1 Corinthians 11:1 NASB)

──────────────── o o o ────────────────

IN SEARCH OF HEROES

Now that I'm older;
in the second half of life,
my ambitions bolder;
children, family and wife.

Different heroes I now claim.
Those I seek to admire.
Their virtues, the same.
Their focus, much higher.

Like knights who did battle,
Fear, temptation and doubt,
for those thought just chattel,
fought day in and day out.

In Arthur's time they too,
did face many a foe:
dragon, warlock, and shrews;
temptresses from below—

failed crops, Black Death, road thugs—
and some neighbor's loose wife.
They fought; they could not shrug,
for their few they'd give their life.

The kings' and knights' deeds done
were heroic, it's true.
But just give the common
Medieval man his due.

Their names and deeds not told
in tall or lustrous tale.
But brought to me, my small fold,
a more important scale.

Behind

How different would our history textbooks read, if written by God, truly chronicling the important events and people throughout the ages? If the true measure of any activity is what is left over after the activity is complete—if the Mona Lisa is the measure of value for Leonardo's brushwork—then, what will be the measure of all of our efforts? What will be left over at the end of all things?

Who is the dependable source for valuing all things? Who is worthy of directing our search for heroes? There is only One who has been there to the end of all things, and came to us to reveal what will be of value in that end and, therefore, worth pursuing now. The good news is He has come, and has demonstrated to us through His life and death on the cross, the true measures of a hero. He showed us those measures are within the reach of every common man, of every age.

It was my desire in this poem to honor the common man hero.

C.S. Lewis put it this way in his sermon, *The Weight of Glory*, "There are no ordinary people. You have never talked to a mere mortal. Nations, cultures, arts, civilizations - these are mortal, and their life is to ours as the life of a gnat. But it is immortals whom we joke with, work with, marry, snub, and exploit - immortal horrors or everlasting splendors."

I have always been stirred by the radically counter-culture statements of Jesus regarding the Kingdom, leadership and greatness.

Whoever humbles himself like this child is the greatest in the kingdom of heaven. (Matthew 18:4 ESV)

Truly, I say to you, among those born of women there has arisen no one greater than John the Baptist. Yet the one who is least in the kingdom of heaven is greater than he.

(Matthew 11:11 ESV)

And he sat down and called the twelve. And he said to them, "If anyone would be first, he must be last of all and servant of all." (Mark 9:35 ESV)

These, and verses like them, inspire me to search for a different kind of hero than the world offers, and to rethink how I look at being a "common man."

————————————— o o —————————————

Between

But the LORD said to Samuel, "Do not look on his appearance or on the height of his stature, because I have rejected him. For the LORD sees not as man sees: man looks on the outward appearance, but the LORD looks on the heart."
(1 Samuel 16:7 ESV)

Spend some time thinking about how valuable you can be to the lives of those around you. How does loving and serving others impact their eternal destiny? That is something worth fighting for. How might God be leading you to be a hero for someone today and is He drawing you towards searching for some new heroes yourself—ones you can admire and imitate, as they imitate Christ?

————————————— o o o —————————————

AMBITION

Just gone midnight,
not halfway done,
hope to finish
before the sun.

Just gone midnight,
still not quite home,
fighting fatigue,
my mind will roam.

Just gone midnight,
can't get to sleep,
so much I've sown,
afraid I'll reap.

Just gone midnight,
again I wait,
in empty bed,
my selfish fate.

Behind

The origin of the poem, *Ambition*, stems from a short phrase I discovered because of my love of travel.

My affection probably predated those family cross country excursions in the Airstream. My wonder lust has its roots in the stories my Dad used to tell. He was an Airstream sales manager, and as such, had been all over the US (and overseas). He loved to bring back stories of fascinating people and places. Each year, he and my mother would take off for a week to some exotic land to attend Airstream's international sales convention. Year after year, I remember waiting with great anticipation for them to return home. Late into the night my sister, brother and I would sit up, opening souvenir gifts, looking at pictures and postcards and listening to stories of the fascinating places and interesting people they had seen.

Over those years, I built up so many visions of travel adventure and wonder, that once my own traveling days began, I seemed to have a never ending supply of positive anticipation toward going on a trip—any trip. Now, even when the inevitable adult travel "disasters" occurs—losing luggage or missing a flight, I don't seem to mind. They really are to me the spice that adds flavor to the stories that I tell my children when I get home.

I particularly love to travel to England. I love its history and people very much. I enjoy the adventure of experiencing the differences in our cultures, customs and habits, especially the differences in words and phrases in every day conversations. That brings me to the origin of this poem.

Back at home while listening to a BBC podcast, during my drive to work, my attention was grabbed by a phrase the announcer used to introduce a program. Each BBC Worldnews program starts out with, "Welcome to the latest global news, recorded at (time of day) on (day of the week). I am (presenter's name) with a selection of highlights from across the BBC World Service." The phrase used to indicate the time was, "Welcome to the latest global news, recorded 'just gone midnight' on . . ." kept repeating in my head."

Over the next couple days, I mulled over that phrase again and again, until feelings of dark sadness, loneliness, quiet urgency, pain and regret filled the atmosphere around the line, *just gone midnight*. Specific scenes and images of our culture's plight emerged. The repeated original line, many of those emotions and four of those images, became the poem - *Ambition*.

———————————————————— o o ————————————————————

Between

A Song of Ascents, of Solomon.
Unless the LORD builds the house,
They labor in vain who build it;
Unless the LORD guards the city,
The watchman keeps awake in vain.

It is vain for you to rise up early,
To retire late,
To eat the bread of painful labors;
For He gives to His beloved even in his sleep.
(Psalm 127:1, 2 NASB)

Are we living life out of balance, out of whack, working so hard and aiming at the wrong target? Are we listening to the wrong sources and being driven by hollow ambitions? There is the admirable drive, that spurs us on to do what needs to be done in times of necessity. There is honor there. But how much of our culture's driven-ness simply comes from misguided ambition? Spend some time meditating on the poem and Psalm 127:1, 2 side by side. Enjoy listening for additional things God might reveal to you.

———————————————— o o o ————————————————

UNEXPECTED

Deadbolt snap,
front door swoosh,
screen door scringe
and I step out

to cross the porch
and down the stairs,
to waiting car
and off to work.

But on this cold, dark mid-October morn,
as orange light slips between the slats
and dissolves unnoticed to black below,

I'm stopped in my routine
by beauty unexpected.

Shyly in the dark,
between proud pickets,
a small red rose
floats within the void.

She's waiting patiently to open
to promised coming sun,
felt before
but never seen.

Unexpected beauty.

To take a stand,
in the light,
amidst the dark.

Against the fall—
to shine.

But I, cocooned
in my routine,
must miss
the moment.

She will open alone,
with no one to see,
but her Creator,
the saints
and all the hosts of heaven
shouting out His name.

I move on…

Behind

Normally, when I leave for work, it's one smooth motion; out my front door, turn to the right, and by the time I reach the railing gap at the top of the steps that descend to the paving stones, my eyes have adjusted. I can then navigate the stairs, work my keys into the car door and the ignition and I am gone. But not this time. My eyes were sweeping, clicking along from rail to rail, like a little kid running a stick along a fence. Suddenly my daily routine lost all momentum. Frozen, my gaze was fixed on unexpected beauty. A small, shy red rose bud was floating between two slats, just beyond the boundary of the bright border that normally robs all the attention from anything beyond.

I just stood there. I could not take my eyes off of the rose. Not only was she defying the monopoly of the porch railing for the right to shine and be seen, but she was ignoring the demands of the season. It was no longer spring or summer. By what authority was this fragile one daring to stand and bloom? The rest of her kind had the good sense and politeness to wither, give up and die. Didn't she know she was too late? The time for such boldness had passed.

The next thing I knew, the spell was broken. I came back to myself and my routine. I pulled out my phone and tried to capture the moment with a digital photograph. Naturally, try as I might, each image seemed flat; a poor reflection of the strong innocence before me. I could not capture the feeling of wonder I was experiencing. Quickly, before the light changed, I called my wife out to share the scene. Planting a kiss on her cheek, I left her there to soak it in, and I was off to work.

All during my drive I was captivated by the joy of the rose and haunted with a mixture of my own thankfulness and regret. Often that day, I returned to my computer to write this poem.

Between

Slow down a bit today and take the time to look around you for the beauty and boldness God has placed around you. If something catches your eye, take the time to linger and listen.

If, in your attentiveness, He shows you someone exhibiting the unexpected beauty of   taking a stand, pray about how God might lead you to respond.

Later, if you want to linger a little longer, grab your Bible and lay Ephesians 6:10-24 next to the poem. Read them together and see what connections God brings to your mind.

Therefore, take up the full armor of God, so that you will be able to resist in the evil day, and having done everything, to stand firm. (Ephesians 6:13 NASB)

———————————— o o o ————————————

AN IRISHMAN DOES THE TELL

When me "I" was me.
Me alone.
I was free.

Free to be.
Free to be me.
Free as stone;

selfish, afraid and alone.

So, over the years,
I filled up my house;

friends, family,
children,
neighbors
and spouse.

I worked hard to impress
with things that mattered;

job titles,
cars, trophies,
and me wallet
was fatter.

Still something was wrong,
something inside,

an emptiness,
people
and things

could not hide.

Then in the midst
of my full empty life,
the flipside of grace
invaded my strife.

When He die for me,
I forgiven be.
Me debt was paid.
He set me free.

But more than free
and empty be,
more than cleansed
and made amends.

Yes, died to free,
but raised was He,
to take His place
on heaven's lee.

Seated there
first born,
new race.

Then sent His Spirit
to fill
me space.

Came in
re-rooted,
revived alive.

Cleansed to
fill
me empty "I".

Now me, "I",
no longer
ME,

but henceforth
and forever
WE.

Behind

This poem was triggered by a simple comment that a friend of mine made, years ago, at the end of a phone conversation. It was just a little line, but for me, it was a spark that God used to fan into a flame that is still burning within me. It was a slight variation on the common phrase, "Well, I've got to go, talk to you later.", but it was to make a big change in my life.

Years ago my friend, Gene, moved from where we both were living in Southern California to upstate New York. We've stayed in touch, mainly through the occasional "catch me up" phone call. Gene ended one such call by saying, "Well, Jesus and I are going upstairs now to fix a door." After I hung up, I thought to myself, *What did he say?* I smiled. That phrase has continued to echo through my soul. It has slowly gathered weight and significance by the addition of bible verses and experiences. It has drawn forward moments out of my past with a new clarity of connection, namely, the thought that, all the time, everywhere I go, I am never alone – "I equals We." There is always We - Jesus and me.

The Apostle Paul said it this way;

…and it is no longer I who live, but Christ lives in me; and the life which I now live in the flesh I live by faith in the Son of God, who loved me and gave Himself up for me.
(Galatians 2:20 NASB)

The distinction between the pronouns in that verse have become so important to me. When I look toward the future, my hope is no longer in Kirk (I alone) achieving, but in Jesus (in me) achieving, Jesus living out His life through me (I=We).

The admonitions in the bible to walk by faith, as well as walking in the Spirit, have taken on new reality for me. It is no longer me trying to live, to feel alive, significant, safe, or

important by achievement, or collecting things or even people for myself.
Between

This is how we know that we live in him and he in us: He has given us of his Spirit. (1 John 4:13 NIV)

If you are a Christian, you have Christ in you. You are no longer just you. How will you experience and express that "I equals We" today?

○ ○ ○

DISTRACTIONS

Why do I go to the river at night?
They are all there in the city by day?

Because, when I lay on my back
on that flat, floating roof,
I see them and hear what they say.

In the busy and bright,
blocked by the blue,
the effect of the big one hides them from view.

Even at night,
when it should be alright,
Edison and Ad-men distract our sight.

What we've invented
profits the lie;
illuminates earth and obscures the sky.

But not out from the city,
suburbs and towns,
not out on the water; no others around.

Back in the rush,
you don't notice them glisten.
Here you can't help but look up and listen.

Listen to the story,
centuries old,
truth frozen in motion, silent and bold.

He's as constant
in your life,
wherever you are.

So go to your river
and quiet your soul.
Listen through the clutter
and come back whole.

Behind

Distractions dates back to the 1980s and a very special place—a flat floating roof. The roof was the top of one of seven houseboats that made up a most unique summer camp ministry.

For one week each summer, the house boats became home for twelve students and a couple of adult leaders. After the houseboats were loaded, and with a sleek ski boat in tow, we would drive to a secluded cove for our first night's stay. After dinner, we gathered on the top of one of the boats for program time. Under a clear black sky, filled with stars, we worshipped and I shared my traditional message. I started by having the students sit back, look up and listen to the silence of the California River delta.

Every church youth ministry looks for a summer camp experience that will, not only attract students to attend, but also impact their lives in a unique and lasting way. For us, this camp provided that experience. There was no property, no cabins, no swimming pools, no hiking trails, no lodge, no dining hall and no chapel. Only miles of the most beautiful water skiing conditions you could find anywhere.

The message went something like this: "Why do we come to the river each summer? Look up and see what God has made. Take it in. All this week, I invite you, in between the skiing, the swimming, the program and exploring, to take the time to pause and listen. If you do, you may hear from God in ways you never have before. We come to the river to get away from the clutter and distractions of our normal lives and to see things in a different way."

For many of those who came to the Delta and sat on that flat floating roof, their lives were never the same . . .

———————————————————— o o ————————————————————

Between

What is God calling you to do to quiet the noise, to cut through the clutter and spend more time with Him? In your time with the Lord today, here are three verses to enjoy alongside the poem.

But Jesus Himself would often slip away to the wilderness and pray. (Luke 5:16 NASB)

"…and lo, I am with you always, even to the end of the age."
(Matthew 28:20 NASB)

Rejoice evermore. Pray without ceasing. In everything give thanks: for this is the will of God in Christ Jesus concerning you. (1Thessalonians 5:16-18 KJV)

———————————— o o o ————————————

BROKE INTO

**One day at my desk,
my heart broke . . .**

My daughters are away
at college,
on their own—
no, not yet.

The school's watching out for them
to fail
to ask the right questions,
read the fine print.

The broader my vision,
bigger my heart,
the more it is broken,
more set apart.

Set apart from the selfish,
vision expands;
sees so much more
than mere flesh would demand.

Led by His spirit,
see life through new eyes,
He's called us to action,
no longer disguised.

Called us, equipped us,
shows us white fields—
but too much to be done
for even 24/7 to yield.

Hearts break inside us
just like the Son,
till we come to see
that He is the one.

The clearer our vision
of who He is,
the deeper we trust Him
for those who are His.

Then the more the heart heals,
trading pain and remorse
for peace and for gratitude—
all in due course.

The heart's journey from selfish
 to grateful is one,
through tears into trusting,
just like the Son.

Trusting the Father,
so Jesus wept and He slept
and there were still people
not healed in the world.

Love on
dear friends,
                    love on.

      . . . into gratitude.

Behind

One day, while I was sitting at my desk, my three daughters broke my heart. As you grow and the Lord gives you a greater and greater capacity to see with unselfish eyes and love with a true desire to help and care for others, your heart will be broken. Your capacity to see and care will outstrip your capacity to do.

It was during my last daughter, Stefanee's senior year in college, I was doing "what I do." I was helping her wrestle with her school's administration office.

Having sorted things out, again, my mind began to wander. I was thinking about daughters, Nicole, Abree and Stefanee, and about how much I loved them. How I wanted to stay in touch with them and be there for them when they faced all the adult struggles ahead. I knew there would be so many difficult decisions to come, so many choices and requirements, with so little time to properly research all the factors even if they knew where to look and who to trust. Fighting City Hall and wrestling with the bursar's office were the kinds of things I had come to understand and (even at times) enjoy. But there was only so much I could do to protect them against what was ahead. The moment I saw the scope of their needs, my heart broke and the tears began to flow. I was not enough.

As my pain put the world on pause, I heard the voice of God from deep inside. As if to insure the breaking, He said, "You are not enough." My chest tightened. I replied, "I know, I am not enough, but I care so much." He replied, "You love them so much. I love them more. Trust me.

It took such a short period of time for my heart to be *broken into*…..gratitude. I moved quickly from desperately caring, to breaking through, hearing and trusting, and to joy-filled gratitude.

I spent the rest of the morning smiling and so thankful.

———————————————— o o ————————————————

Between

...casting all your care upon Him, for He cares for you.
(1Peter 5:7 NKJV)

We all have people in our lives that we care about. Next to
loving God Himself, our purpose, assignment, commandment
and mission is to "love one another." Has loving ever brought
you to a breaking? If so, you are in good company. Jesus loved
so deeply. Seeing the afflictions suffered by the crowds that
came to hear Him teach, "Jesus wept."

What an amazing and great example. Not only did Jesus weep
for those He loved, but He also trusted God, the Father, enough
to be at peace. "Jesus slept." Jesus was able to walk in peace
and joy because He trusted the Father and knew, if He followed
His Father's lead in everything, it would be enough.

Take some time, today, to lift up, in prayer, those you care
about. If you have burdens you've been carrying for loved
ones, lay 1 Peter 5:7 next to the poem and listen for God's
leading.

———————————————— o o o ————————————————

DIVIDE

For the word of God is living and powerful, and sharper than any two-edged sword, piercing even to the division of soul and spirit....

(Hebrews 4:12 NKJV)

Sever swift, oh sword of God.
Render true this binding blend,
break my murky, mixing sod,
tyranny of soul to end.

Woken, stillborn-slumber done.
Quickened, inner coma flown.
Finished, ancient battle won.
Spirit, please, now, take the throne.

Every day I'll give the lead,
Spirit, then my soul is free,
takes his place like mighty steed,
servant to the rider be.

Sear me sure with light and voice,
open me to make the choice.

Behind

The pendulum of inspiration seems to swing into a fairly steady rhythm between personal experiences and lessons from the written Word. Written roots spring from the Bible, most clearly from Hebrews 4:12, and the book, *The Spiritual Man* by Watchman Nee.

Though the truth is from the Word of God, the urgent sense of desperation in, *Divide,* comes from me. It rises from my own deep fervent calling out to God to set things right in me.

Throughout most of my Christian life, I was unable to understand, let alone, give the lead of my life over to the Holy Spirit. It was not until I read the book, *The Spiritual Man,* that I truly understood the Holy Spirit.

If I had understood, early on, the true nature of what I needed, I would have spontaneously shouted, "do it Word." My spirit, the inner most part of me that communes with God, senses His Presence and leading and is intended (from the beginning) to lead my soul and body.

As I began reading *The Spiritual Man*, my eyes opened to the truth about the nature of Man; what made up the different parts of "me", and why I often experienced confusion and frustration when it came to spiritual things. I started seeing the differences between the various inner parts of me that the Bible speaks about, what their proper roles were and their true functions. I better understood what "walking in the flesh" (being led by soul & body) meant and how destructive this path could be. Then, I experienced amazing times, when my soul, distinctly separated from my spirit, was free to function as it was created to, serving my spirit. My soul could be the expression of God's life, received through my spirit. What a wonderful new life opened up to me!

It was this new understanding and appreciation of the truth in Hebrew 4:12. that was the motivation behind *DIVIDE.*

———————————————— o o ————————————————

Between

Is there an area of your life where you feel out of control? Do you experience your soul (i.e. your mind, will or emotions) dominating your spirit and hampering God's loving leadership from flowing through you? If so, read the poem again as a prayer—asking the Lord to use His word to divide your soul and spirit.

Here are two verses about the soul and spirit to contemplate throughout your day.

Praise the LORD, my soul; all my inmost being, praise his holy name. (Psalm 103:1 NIV)

…for God gave us a spirit not of fear but of power and love and self-control. (2 Timothy 1:7 ESV)

———————————————— o o o ————————————————

ToE

You know all things
about all things
cause all things came
from You.

When I say, "came",
I don't mean brought,
I mean brought forth
from nothing.

When I say, "all",
don't just mean stuff,
mean thoughts behind
the things.

When I say, "things",
I don't mean just
thoughts and stuff
but every step between.

Every atom
and every force
and every source
of every force,

and all the math
that's looking back,
describing all
the hidden facts.

There is nothing
I encounter,
nothing
I will do,

nothing unrelated,
it all
has come
from You.

Everything has purpose,
meaning behind each one.
Every moment is a chance
to listen to the Son.

All answers to discover,
all things we seek to find,
solutions to our problems,
they're all in Him to find.

All are invitations,
calling us back home,
back to the garden,
where we never walk alone.

The One who knows all things,
beckons us to live
conscious of the truth
that only He can give.

Behind

Two components are behind the writing of this poem: one, a thought that helped me keep a, decades old, promise to myself—and two, the simple marching rhythm of the first stanza.

The Thought

Many years ago, I read a small, yet profound, book by a seventeenth century monk named Brother Lawrence. It is a collection of letters, and conversations centered on the goal of his life—to live with a constant awareness of the presence of God. The book is called, *The Practice of the Presence of God.*

After reading that book in my early twenties, and promising myself I would apply it to my life, I struggled with the challenge for decades. My breakthrough finally came a couple years ago with just one simple thought. The thought was this, "God knows all things, about all things, because all things came from Him - ALL THINGS". Nothing is new to Him. Nothing new to us could make Him out-of-date or unconnected, for they are not new to Him.

I had always felt close to God and found it easy to "Practice His Presence" while in church services or during quiet times of bible reading, prayer and worship. But at work, it had been a different story. Often, I would leave, at the end of a long business day, and suddenly be struck by the thought, "Oh, there you are God". God was a separate thing, not present or connected to so much of my world.

I realized that the Holy Spirit was ever present and wanted to be interacting with me about everything. Now I saw why that kind of communication was possible. Because He knew everything about everything. And why not? It all came from Him.

This realization helped me to fulfill the promise I made to myself all those years ago—the promise to apply the precepts of the book to my life. It was the last piece of the puzzle and became the first lines in this poem.

The Rhythm

As the first phrase kept repeating itself in my mind, it became the first stanza and revealed its simple marching rhythm to me. The light marching beat began to carry me along. I heard the repeating, "Da da, Da dum. Da da, Da Dum. Da da, Da dum. Da da". The words started out addressed to God. They were a response to Him, a lifting up of thanks to Him, and an acknowledgment that I could experience His presence with me in all things, because He knows all things.

Oh yes, one more thing! The title. *ToE,* is the academic acronym for the "Theory of Everything".

───────────────── o o ─────────────────

Between

Is there a time of your day when you find it hard to maintain a conscious awareness of the Presence of God? Dedicate this devotional time, today, and perhaps a specific time each day this week, to interacting with God about that space in your life.

Here are some verses on which to meditate.

"… lo, I am with you always, even to the end of the age." (Matthew 28:20 NASB)

"I will ask the Father, and He will give you another Helper, that He may be with you forever; that is the Spirit of truth, whom the world cannot receive, because it does not see Him or know Him, but you know Him because He abides with you and will be in you." (John 14:16-17 NASB)

Rejoice always; pray without ceasing; in everything give thanks; for this is God's will for you in Christ Jesus. (1 Thessalonians 5:16-18 NASB)

Whatever you do, do your work heartily, as for the Lord rather than for men, (Colossians 3:23 NASB)

ooo

THE GLASS BROKE

The glass broke,
one hour before my heart.
The last stroke,
before she slipped away.

The fear spoke,
as if to tear apart.
The dream woke,
before the break of day.

The cruel joke,
"…back to my start."
The fire's smoke,
before her hearth I'll stay!

Behind

This poem owes its start to a mistake— to the misunderstanding of a phrase in a song that caught my ear and moved my heart. My wife, Rachelle, and I were driving in her car one sunny afternoon.

Rachelle always drove when we rode in her baby, our clean little, white, '95 mustang. The radio was on in the background. All of a sudden, my attention was seized by a line in a song. I thought, *Wow, what a cool, haunting line.* I stopped talking and listened to see if the line would repeat in the song, or if the continuing context would fill in the meaning. No, it was gone, but it had sunk in and the words lingered.

When I mentioned it to Rachelle, we both came to realize that we knew the song and interestingly the line I heard was not even in the song.

By the time I wrote the line down, two strong images had formed in my mind. The words and sentiment had become mine. They triggered in me both the image of a sad person, and an old fairytale. With these two, different yet connected, pictures, I started writing one poem that eventually broke into two. This poem is the personal one. That second poem comes later in this collection.

As I wrote the first drafts of *The Glass Broke* I found that the dominant and obvious fairytale connection, though meaningful to me, was getting in the way of a second image I saw. The more personal story pressed on me and would not be crowded out.

○ ○

Between

What story is God showing you, when you read *The Glass Broke*?

John Newton, the eighteenth century author of the song, *Amazing Grace,* put it this way, "My grand point in preaching is to break the hard heart, and to heal the broken one." Are you ready to trust Him in it all?

Below are verses to add to your devotional time. Enjoy!

He heals the brokenhearted
And binds up their wounds. (Psalms 147:3 NASB)

'For I know the plans that I have for you,' declares the LORD, 'plans for welfare and not for calamity to give you a future and a hope...' (Jeremiah 29:11 NASB)

The LORD is near to the brokenhearted
And saves those who are crushed in spirit.
Many are the afflictions of the righteous,
But the LORD delivers him out of them all.
(Psalms 34:18-19 NASB)

"...and He will wipe away every tear from their eyes; and there will no longer be any death; there will no longer be any mourning, or crying, or pain; the first things have passed away." (Revelation 21:4 NASB)

————————————— o o o —————————————

ASSIGNMENT

A cloud is lifting, time to write.
The challenge? How to rhyme
A ballad rhythm poem tonight,
And how the flow to prime.

Well, if I am to write this rhyme
And scribe what's on my heart;
I must away, alone for time
To give my soul a start.

That second stanza's what I wrote
And sent off to some friends
One wrote me back "line three's a 'cheat';
Rewrite to make amends."

Well, if I am to right this rhyme
And work to fix its flaws
I guess I might pick up a book
And read those grammar laws.

I skipped the book and took to pen
I knew what I had meant
I ruminated, "what to say"
And this is what I sent

Well, if I am to write this rhyme
And scribe what's on my heart;
I must withdraw and muse a time
To give my soul a start.

Lou wrote me back, "The rhythm's right,
A ballad true to form.
And now line three is really great;
It more than meets the norm."

Behind

I owe this poem to the challenge of a talented and gracious academic friend. Behind all my poems are the encouragements, advice and insights of many friends, who have informally been my teachers and mentors in what (for me) has never come naturally—writing! I have always had a story to tell, passions to express and creative ideas, solutions and adventures to describe. But to write it out - that's always been a different story.

Over the past few years, off and on, I have been re-studying the rules, all at a layman's pace. I am growing to love it. With poetry, I can study the rules as I have had time. As I try out some of the new things I've learned, forms and patterns of rhythm appear. If they work for me—great—but if not, I break it and follow what seems natural for the specific poem. I love it. As I find my way through the wealth of options in poetry, friends and acquaintances who have been willing to share what they have learned have been invaluable to me.

———————————— o o ————————————

Between

The poem is a wonderful opportunity to practice the maxim, "All life can be devotional." On the surface, there are no spiritual themes in this poem, but still, God is speaking and active in you. Take this opportunity to listen. Read through the poem again with a prayerful attitude of "what do You want to say to me through this piece. There may be scriptures like these that come to mind:

Iron sharpens iron, So one man sharpens another.
(Proverbs 27:17 NASB)

A wise man will hear and increase in learning, And a man of understanding will acquire wise counsel, (Proverbs 1:5 NASB)

Listen to counsel and accept discipline, That you may be wise the rest of your days. (Proverbs 19:20 NASB)

───────────────────── o o o ─────────────────────

A CINDERELLA STORY...

The glass slipper broke,
one hour before my heart.
The clock strikes one, last stroke,
before they said, "...away".

The fear, in dream it spoke,
as if to tear apart.
My tortured mind awoke
before the break of day.

The cruel discovered joke,
"Come meet...back at my start."
They'd hid her note to cloak,
she'd wanted me away.

At last her chimney's smoke
by God, we'll wed today!

        ...for ever after.

Behind

I enjoyed bringing to life another interpretation of the much loved, 17th century folk tale, *Cinderella*. The history of this fable is rich, with many versions and different titles. In France, it was known as, *The Little Glass Slipper*. While I let my mind wonder through the short, and cryptic lines of my poem, I added and changed key words to clarify and reveal my own new telling of *A Cinderella Story*.

───────────────── ○ ○ ─────────────────

Between

"My sheep hear My voice, and I know them, and they follow Me; (John 10:27 NASB)

If God is speaking and I am listening, can I hear Him speak to me through a poem birthed out of a children's fairytale? The challenge is not whether the poem's content is profound enough to communicate a deep truth from God, or even whether the poem is crafted skillfully enough to draw you in. The challenge is: am I listening?

If we are to be people of God, walking in fellowship with Him and following His lead we must learn to listen for His voice and practice remaining in His presence, even when the "things" before us do not, of themselves, assist us to do so. If we limit ourselves to expecting Him to speak only through "great" sermons, and styles of worship that are for us "moving," we will miss out on so much from Him.

I offer you this challenge, especially when circumstances are distracting, practice hearing God through all things.

Re-read *A Cinderella Story*, pausing often and asking, "Lord, what do you have for me in this part of the poem today?"

———————————————— o o o ————————————————

REAPING THE NIGHT WIND

Now I lay me down to sleep,
I find no rest, through cracks it seeps.
If I shall die before I wake,
all that I've built, cold time will take.

If, "Nothing after death" is true,
no pleasure, joy or peace is due.
If on the other side, He's real,
all that I've done my fate will seal.

As I drift off, these thoughts drift in,
carried on some dark foul wind.
My doors are shut and windows fast.
Still through my soul, deep shadows cast.

Each morning comes with less relief.
Now days are minefields, night's a thief.

Behind

Reaping the Night Wind was inspired by an eerie photograph I took late one night, while driving home from work. It was a dark, hazy, starless night. The moon was full and I was in a hurry to get home. But on my way, a striking image caught my eye. As I made a left turn down an old farm road, out the driver side window, I saw an old, tall, windmill sweep across the face of the stark winter moon. The passing silhouette of fan tail towered over tall trees in a hazy mist. It sent a chill down the back of my neck. I hit the brakes, slapped the car into reverse, and backed it up until I found that perfect spot, I grabbed my phone and started taking pictures.

Later that night, at home, I was scrolling through the images, hoping I could find that feeling again and there it was. One of the photographs had captured the moment, and I began to write. The title came first. A combination of the purpose and the activating force behind the windmill, the planting and harvesting nature of the farming culture and the Poe-like foreboding evoked by the photograph resulted in the phrase *Reaping the Night Wind.*

As I was getting tired, my mind drifted this poem into two directions. One, the growing fear and restlessness of a soul without God, obsessively looking into the two bleak eventualities of its future, and two, the contrasting hope of the nursery rhyme; "When I lay me down to sleep...." The result was this little poem of warning.

––––––––––––––––––––––––––– o o –––––––––––––––––––––––––––

Between

Have you come to the place in life where you are no longer afraid of the dark? Is the issue of what awaits you on the other side of death a settled thing in your life? What a wonderful place to be, in life, when the thought of death no longer robs us of sleep, when we can receive that gift of peace Jesus offers us:

"Peace I leave with you; My peace I give to you; not as the world gives do I give to you. Do not let your heart be troubled, nor let it be fearful." (John 14:27 NASB)

What security there is in knowing that He loves us and has gone to prepare a future for us:

"In My Father's house are many dwelling places; if it were not so, I would have told you; for I go to prepare a place for you. If I go and prepare a place for you, I will come again and receive you to Myself, that where I am, there you may be also." (John 14:2-3 NASB)

Spend some time today thanking God for the peace His promises bring when we trust in Him. Ask God to give you a sensitivity to others around you who may not have that peace. Pray about being ready and willing to be used by Him to share the good news with someone who is still in that painful place of fear about their future.

---------------------------------- o o o ----------------------------------

DIFFRACTION

Through a crack in an old tool shed,
a young beam of light appeared.
He slowly moved across the floor,
then up upon the owner's gear.

Pushing back the dark inside,
dust appeared, it danced and swirled.
Finally to a prism glass,
pushing through, rainbow'd the world.

In the razored, polished wedge,
unseen silent hammers fell,
bent and broke and split the sun.
What happened there, who can tell?

Out flowed every virtue bright:
truth, and justice, courage, care,
mercy, forgiveness, and grace,
were there.

Every hue and shade between,
the full spectrum of love was seen.
Now we look back, up the stream,
through the prism, along the beam.

Up to the source from whence He came,
shows us the love that bears The Name.

Behind

The inspiration for the poem, *Diffraction,* came from an essay written by C.S. Lewis entitled *Meditation in a Toolshed.*

This short, three page piece, is about the radical difference in experience and insight between looking along a beam of light (from the edge or the inside) and looking at the same beam from outside.

Through the poem, I am able to see my own version of the Lewis tool shed. I can envision light piercing the shed and illuminating the dust in the air, as Lewis described. But then, perhaps from an image of my childhood, the light moves along all the floor, up a rough 4 x 4 leg and begins a trek over dust-covered tools laying upon a table. It lingers—hidden for a time, then progresses like one climbing on split and fallen rocks, crowding an uncleared ancient hillside.

There in the midst of all the drab clutter, right in the path of the beam, on the far edge of the flat surface summit of a hollow, peeled paint can, a clear glass prism stands upright alone. The small footprint of the beam seems to slow and hesitate along the dented rim. Once the cold, sharp, vertical crystal wedge is reached, the beam stands tall and presses in, now resolute in motion. Quickly from base to point, He lit up the thin edge of the tall triangle with white fire. He pushed on past, in and through, then burst out the other side and rainbow'd the room!

What I understood was love coming in and breaking out across our world. Love through *Diffraction.*

———————————————— o o ————————————————

Between

In the upper room, among the last things Jesus said to His disciples before his death, was this:

"This is My commandment, that you love one another, just as I have loved you. (John 15:12 NASB)

"Greater love has no one than this, that one lay down his life for his friends." (John 15:13 NASB)

Today, I invite you to read the poem, *Diffraction,* and also John 1:1-9 and John 8:12.

Try the C.I.A. Bible study method here:

C - What is He saying (Cez)?
I - What is He implying (Implies)?
A - How is He calling you to Apply it in your life and when?

———————————————— o o o ————————————————

EAST WIND

The east wind chills
as it sweeps out
the scars of the
beautiful surface,
still new.

He's opening
the ice rink alone…

Forty three seasons,
she'd always found a way
to be there by his side,
that is until today.

None of them
will notice.
They'll all just
pass on through.

No secret spices
in the cider,
and store bought
cakes will do.

Little touches missing,
no rose in his lapel.
The little ones with bruises,
who will they run and tell?

She knew them all,
that's why they came.
No more favorite pairs
set out by name.

He worries, will
the new girl show,
and will she be
as kind?

Can't wait any longer,
the ice, it must be done.
He'll leave the side door open,
won't know if she's begun.

So much is out of our control.
Try as we might, won't do.
So much we treasure, lost,
but some things can be made new.

He guides the great Zambonie,
and heals the ice once more.
The sun streaks through the buildings,
and a light comes through the door.

The rink is opened right on time.
In line the people stand—they came.
He rounds the corner of the shop,
and hears them call his name.

He smells hot cider brewing,
and fresh cakes are baking near.
Turns the final corner,
and drops a single tear.

The skates are on the counter,
each pair by name in rows.
The new girl holds the gate.
Each patron holds a rose.

Behind

The story I came to tell in, *East Wind,* is one born out of faithfulness, loss, sadness, and the healing power of love quietly expressed. The scene itself stems from the years that I was responsible for the care of an ice rink, and yes, I am counted among the small number of human beings who have driven a Zamboni.

The character of the old rink manager is a tribute to my maternal grandfather—a stoic, strong and faithful man. He exuded solid values forged in the great depression; husband of just one wife, faithful to his church, the Word and one company, from which he retired after thirty-five years of service. He was the parts manager for an International Harvester repair shop until the day he died at the age of 84 in 1989. In his last years, he could still tell you the part numbers for many of the International trucks used in World War II.

He and my grandmother, were the kind of people who never put on airs or made a big show of things. But once they were gone, people were quick to tell how much they meant to them and what an impact their quiet faithfulness and love had on their lives. I still run into people who knew them and tell me how much they miss Robert and Elizabeth Applegate.

My grandparents, and the many faithful, quiet, godly couples of that generation, were the inspiration for *East Wind.*

---------------------------------- o o ----------------------------------

Between

When is it right to jump ship and change jobs, schools, careers or spouses?

What makes it possible to stick it out when times get really tough? Where do you find the courage to hold on and push through each drought to the next spring rain?

When we look to the temporal things of this life, like job, achievement, school, kids, spouse, etc., for our core fulfillment, identity, or security, can they really bear the weight of a lifetime? Is the only alternative, now-a-days, to follow the cultural trend of jumping fences until we end up alone in the last empty field?

What do you draw from the following verse about how we can stay through the tough times?

And my God will supply all your needs according to His riches in glory **in Christ Jesus.** (Philippians 4:19 NASB)

What actions will you take as a result of the poem and scripture combined?

———————————————— o o o ————————————————

FROZEN IN THE FALL

I thought to myself one autumn day,
When from this tree, I'm free,
I'll finally reach the solid ground
and Wind will hold no sway on me.

Then finally, for my mates and me,
our chance for freedom came.
Released from the confines of the crowd,
on the real world we'd stake a claim.

We told ourselves it happened in the dark.
When out of sight those other trusting fools,
content to fall upon the top of grass,
exposed, would be caught up and blow away.

Instead, we dove for the grey, flat, walkers
path. We hit that ground and we hunkered down.
Out of the reach of Wind. We waited for
the change; for roots to stay or legs to walk around.

As we guessed, when Sun went down Rain did come.
Now, we'd see her soften earth or change our frames.
Confident as Water rose, we stayed put.
But instead of soft change, came cold hard shame.

While those we thought were fools saw morning thaw,
my mates and me lie frozen in the fall.

Behind

On a snowless, bitter, cold December morning—the kind of day a blanket of snow would make all the chill seem more worthwhile, I was crunching the frost, slowly navigating the frozen sidewalks. While working on keeping my balance, eyes fixed on the slick path, an assortment of brown, red and amber leaves laid staring up at me through a half inch of ice. They caught my attention and sympathy.

Like flowers plucked and pressed under glass, these leaves still seemed young and fresh, frozen in time. Most of the fallen leaves outside my office building just sat there, waiting for wind or rake on the bed of nails that was the frosty lawn around the base of the big tree. It came to mind how these few renegades had taken a different path than all their kin. I worked my phone out of my pocket, selected the appropriate lens, and began snapping portraits of these sidewalk rebels.

That night, after I got home, I reviewed the images, chose three likely leaf friends and pieced them together in a fitting collage. The trio caught my imagination and my memory. I started to write their story, imagining, in my mind, their ill-fated attempt at independence and fame. As I did, I found many points of connection with my own journey, growing up, thinking my friends and I knew more than our elders—even though they had seen many seasons, rains and frozen mornings after a fall.

———————————————— o o ————————————————

Between

In our culture, where the young rebel is praised and the elderly are often set aside and their wisdom not honored or sought after, is it any wonder we can easily find ourselves frozen in a fall. Who are the elderly in your life, older in the faith, whom God has placed around you to help you grow, learn and navigate the difficult, slippery seasons? Pray for God's leading as to how to bless your elders and humbly take advantage of their presence in your life.

" 'Stand up in the presence of the aged, show respect for the elderly and revere your God. I am the LORD.' "
(Leviticus 19:32 NIV)

The hoary head (gray hair) [is] a crown of glory, [if] it be found in the way of righteousness. (Provebs 16:31 KJV)

---------------------------------- o o o ----------------------------------

STEEL BREAD CRUMBS

Backfire'n bug on the Back Bay road.
Ragtop down, burned high, then low.
Feather weight Fiat with the 8-track stowed
under seat, blaring Beach Boys, "Let's Go"!

Number 10 Chevy, riding high and green,
long bed, straight shell, bench seat scene.
'68 brown bug, small wheel turns,
lock-to-lock quick, jacked up she churns.

'73 Thing, when she's all stripped down
she'll climb a wall, deep water won't drown.
'67 Vee Dub camper van:
live, surf, road trip'n still a fan.

Datsun 2000, rice rocket, pre Z.
Smoked that Alpha as she topped Jamboree
Big black Cadillac, dad's hand-me down.
Cruisin' like a mobster without a crown.

Green Pinto wagon, threw the papers at night,
tossed 'em out quick before the morning light.
Fiat 600 with the suicide doors,
starter pull lever, seats hinged to the floor.

Chrysler 300 each bench fits four,
hood like a table and the trunk fits more.
'73 Impala, 'nother big green score,
leaded gas guzzler don't see no more.

'69 Austin American,
two speed auto, drive'n fast as I can.
Two MG's, "No, B's, not A's."

One ran, one parts, broke most days
Such was the trail of my American youth,
junk yard dreams, chasing after the truth—

look'n
for
me,

until I found,

steel icons in cool marques
aren't who we are or who we'll be.
What truly makes us come alive
is how we love, not what we drive.

Behind

Yes, during the first five years, or so, of my driving youth, I owned all those cars. From my sixteenth birthday, in 1976, until a couple years into my first marriage (around 1981), I owned over fifteen cars. I slept cars, ate cars, talked cars and dreamed cars—all the time. I had two to three feet high stacks of car magazines in my bedroom.

I memorized specifications and performance data of my favorite brands and models. I prided myself on being able to name almost any car on the road, mainly the cool ones. Sports cars were my favorite. I could tell you the model year of a passing car from the slightest distinguishing body style eliminate or trim variation. One of the most significant rites of passage moments in my youth came when I bet my Dad ten bucks that the car we both spotted was a 260z rather than a 240z. I won. I knew, right then, that I was becoming a man.

Bench racing (talking about cars) was how my friends and I connected and spent most of our time. For hours, no matter what we were doing, we would show off for each other by displaying our encyclopedic knowledge about cool automobiles. We were always trying to outdo each other. The more hot cars we spotted, the crazier tales we could tell about the daring (dangerous) driving stunts, the more points we would score and the better we felt about ourselves.

I not only talked about cars, I repaired cars and bought and sold them, a lot. Not because I liked those parts of the car game, but because I could not afford the cars I really wanted or even ones in good condition. And I certainly could not pay someone else to maintain or fix them. I spent a lot of time in the garage, not building up the car of my design dreams, but simply to keep them running.

In a short time, I would get tired of one, or it would fall apart. I then sold it and bought another "project." I often rushed out to show off my latest acquisition to my friends, told them of the great deal I struck and the plans I had to customize her. Then, with the cash I had left over, from my part time minimum wages, (after gas, food and dating expenses), I would head off to the parts store, or junk yard to buy what I needed. With parts in hand, it was time to grab my tools and dive in. All fixed up, I would drive her until she fell apart and the cycle would start all over again.

Throughout high school and a bit beyond, cars weren't something I just drove. They were a big part of who I was, or thought I was in front of my peers.

Between

How much of our life—our energy, time and expectations are spent building our personal brand? Is it not a search for, or an attempt to build, who we are, when we attach ourselves to current popular cultural icons? One of my brands-of-choice, while growing up, was "car guy". Others included water polo player, surfer, and even church youth student leader.

As I have gotten older, I hope I have not just replaced those brands of my youth with more adult ones; software developer, event planner, latest gadget guy, writer, etc. Instead, I trust there has been a core shift in the source of my identity—away from the external icons, as beautiful and powerful as they can feel, to the true source of personal identity—purpose and meaning in Jesus Christ.

I still appreciate an automobile's ability to reflect, embody and communicate beauty, character, style, power and personality. But now that I have come to know Jesus in me and who I am in

153

Him, I am growing to no longer rely on those externals to define me before my peers.

Are there shifts that you sense need to be made in your search for identity?

For we are His workmanship, created in Christ Jesus for good works, which God prepared beforehand so that we would walk in them. (Ephesians 2:10 NASB)

Therefore if you have been raised up with Christ, keep seeking the things above, where Christ is seated at the right hand of God. Set your mind on the things above, not on the things that are on earth. For you have died and your life is hidden with Christ in God. When Christ, Who is our life, is revealed, then you also will be revealed with Him in glory. (Col 3:1-4 NASB)

---

o o o

BOWING TO THE ONE

Shakespeare once said that, "All the world's a stage,
and all the men and women merely players."
Then who, on earth, are we performing for?

We enter and we exit off the stage,
and in between, we learn to play our parts
with fans and hecklers filling every scene.

We work the stage from left and right, from drop
to footlights, plus the waiting wings. We feed
on lines and cues, and play the company.

But all the while, we do neglect the house.

At first, the doctor wakes us, parents fill
the scene. Then on to play with mates our age,
more difficult to please. Next comes our peers,
and classes filled with critics—cruel and kind.

We graduate to bosses, spouse and kids.
Then clients, rivals, villains and good friends
will fill the cast. The script ends. One by one,
our fellow actors leave the stage, and we

are left alone. Bright beams go out. We turn
upstage to bow. Downstage there comes a glow,
though different now. We turn to see the why.
The stage is dark; fourth wall* of light is gone.

Astonished now, we find the rumors are
so true. For there is lit an empty hall.
Wait, there, a single seat is occupied.
T'was our rehearsal and audition. Done.

We see it now. We're bowing to the One

*Fourth Wall = stage opening toward the audience & bright stage lights.

Behind

There are three acts to the background of this final poem.

Act 1: The scene opens with me driving to work, early in the morning on a long straight road, ironically named, "Sundown Lane." My attention is captured by a large dead tree on my left. Normally, I passed this lone giant without a thought. In a flash, I wonder how it would look in the foreground of the beautifully developing sunrise I saw in my rear view mirror.

Just past the tree, I turned left, across the yellow line, and pulled off the pavement. Jumping out of my car, I lined up the fullness of these gnarled bare branches, just to the left of the waking sun. I started taking pictures. As I frame the scene for another shot, I notice that the posture of this huge character looks like an actor, flamboyantly bowing, to the sun. Curtain.

Act 2: The curtain rises. The scene is later that night and I am sitting in my living room, sorting through the images from the day. I find the one I am looking for—the big dead tree, bowing to the sun. As I am drawn into the picture, a title pops into my head, *Bowing to the One,* which triggers the memory of a phrase an old mentor of mine used to say.

> "Live your life like there is only one chair in the audience."
> Chuck Miller, Ph.D.

Act 3: With the title and theme in hand, all that was left to complete the piece was form and plot. These were soon provided by the Bard, himself, (Shakespeare). I was lead to his play, *As You Like It,* Act II, Scene VII, and the famous passage starting with, "All the world's a stage…" Then, following his form and plot, I completed my poem as a tribute Chuck, Shakespeare, my fellow actors on the stage and the One in the one chair in the audience!

The End!

Between

We are so influenced by those around us. It is said that it's not what we think of ourselves or what others think of us that matters, but what we think others think of us. When all is said and done, it is what God thinks about us that really matters. He should be the One we are all playing (living) for!

How will you be *Bowing to the One* today?

For am I now seeking the favor of men, or of God? Or am I striving to please men? If I were still trying to please men, I would not be a bond-servant of Christ. (Galatians 1:10 NASB)

And there is no creature hidden from His sight, but all things are open and laid bare to the eyes of Him with whom we have to do. (Hebrews 4:13 NASB)

———————————— o o o ————————————

CPSIA information can be obtained
at www.ICGtesting.com
Printed in the USA
LVOW10s0242211216
518186LV00002B/660/P